Dear Reader

To help us in our future planning of *Day by Day with God*, please take a few moments to c[...] by 31 October to: BRF, FR[...] [req]uired if posted in the UK). Th[...] [assi]stance.

Your Name: _____

Your Address: _____

Town: _____

Postcode: _____ [Country]: _____

Tel: _____ Fax: _____ Email: _____

Denomination: _____

1. **Age:** 16–25 ❑   26–40 ❑   41–60 ❑   60+ ❑

2. **Marital status:** Single ❑   Married ❑   Divorced ❑   Widowed ❑

3. **Do you have children?**   YES ❑   NO ❑

    If YES, are any under 11 years old?   YES ❑   NO ❑

4. **Do you have responsibilities in your church in any of the following areas?** (Please tick all that apply.)
   PCC or eldership   ❑   Pastoral care   ❑
   Sunday School   ❑   Administration   ❑
   Bible study groups   ❑
   Other (please specify) _____

5. **Which Christian magazines and/or newspapers do you read regularly?**

6. **How do you obtain your notes?**   By subscription from BRF ❑   via someone in your church ❑   from your local bookshop ❑

7. **Please indicate which (if any) Bible reading notes you have tried other than *Day by Day with God*:**

8. **Do you like the current format (page size) of *Day by Day with God*?**
   YES ❑   NO ❑

   If NO, should it be bigger? ❑   smaller? ❑

9. **Would you like more themes/topics covered (e.g. Work, Women in the Bible, Prayer) alongside the series of readings from particular books of the Bible?**   YES ❑   NO ❑

If YES, can you suggest themes for future issues?

___

10. Is the length of contributions right (i.e. usually one to two weeks of readings from each writer), or would you prefer longer contributions from fewer writers, or more writers writing less?

    Too long ❏   About right ❏   Too short ❏

11. From the following list, please rate the five most helpful contributors from the team who write for *Day by Day with God*.

Beryl Adamsbaum	___	Janet Lumb	___
Diana Archer	___	Hilary McDowell	___
Celia Bowring	___	Bridget Plass	___
Anne Coomes	___	Elaine Pountney	___
Ann England	___	Wendy Pritchard	___
Rosemary Green	___	Christina Rees	___
Pat Harris	___	Mary Reid	___
Margaret Killingray	___	Alie Stibbe	___
Jennifer Rees Larcombe	___	Ann Warren	___
Christine Leonard	___		

12. Do you have any suggestions for future contributors to *Day by Day with God*?

___

13. At the end of the notes are a number of order forms. Have you ever used these to:
    a) Take out a Gift Subscription? YES ❏ NO ❏
    b) Order a book advertised in the Magazine? YES ❏ NO ❏

14. Do you read the Magazine section?   YES ❏ NO ❏

15. Do you have any suggestions for features/articles in future issues of the Magazine?

___

16. Would you like to receive the BRF and Christina Press catalogues?   YES ❏ NO ❏

17. Would you consider giving a gift subscription to *Day by Day with God* to a friend or relative?   YES ❏ NO ❏

Thank you for your help. Please send this form to BRF, FREEPOST, Oxford, OX4 5BR (no stamp required if posted in the UK)

Day by Day With God

Bible Readings for Women

SEPTEMBER–DECEMBER 1999

Christina Press
Bible Reading Fellowship
Crowborough/Oxford

Copyright © 1999 Christina Press and BRF

BRF, Peter's Way, Sandy Lane West, Oxford, OX4 5HG

First published in Great Britain 1999

ISBN 1 84101 058 8

Jacket design: Bookprint Creative Services, Eastbourne

Trade representation in UK:
Lion Publishing plc, Peter's Way, Sandy Lane West,
Oxford OX4 5HG

Distributed in New Zealand by:
Scripture Union Wholesale, PO Box 760, Wellington

Distributed in South Africa by:
Struik Book Distributors, PO Box 193, Maitland 7405

Acknowledgments
Scriptures quoted from the Good News Bible published
by The Bible Societies/HarperCollins Publishers Ltd,
UK © American Bible Society 1966, 1971, 1976, 1992,
used with permission.

The Living Bible copyright © 1971 by Tyndale House
Publishers.

Scriptures from The Revised Standard Version of the
Bible, copyright © 1946, 1952, 1971 by the Division of
Christian Education of the National Council of the
Churches of Christ in the USA, used by permission.
All rights reserved.

Scriptures from The New Revised Standard Version of
the Bible, Anglicized Edition, copyright © 1989, 1995
by the Division of Christian Education of the National
Council of the Churches of Christ in the USA, used by
permission. All rights reserved.

Scripture quotations taken from *The Holy Bible, New
International Version*, copyright © 1973, 1978, 1984 by
International Bible Society. Used by permission of
Hodder & Stoughton Ltd. All rights reserved. 'NIV' is
a registered trademark of International Bible Society.
UK trademark number 1448790.

Extracts from the Authorized Version of the Bible (The
King James Bible), the rights in which are vested in the
Crown, are reproduced by permission of the Crown's
Patentee, Cambridge University Press.

p. 107: 'and that will be heaven' by Evangeline
Paterson, used with permission.

Printed in Great Britain
by Caledonian Book Manufacturing International,
Glasgow

Contents

The Editor writes...

Day by Day with God has been with us now for two years and I have been on the receiving end of many encouraging comments from women who have been using the notes and found them helpful and relevant in their daily lives. Always a letter arrives on my desk, or someone phones or speaks to me at a time when encouragement is needed—and I thank the Lord for this. If you have any ideas, suggestions or comments on the notes or the magazine section, please do write to me. I have already found input from readers (positive and negative!) helpful as I plan ahead.

In God's hands...

One of our readers handed a copy of *Day by Day with God* to someone who was ill, not realizing that she was due to go to hospital for tests that very day. The Bible passage was totally appropriate for that lady's circumstances—'Do not fear, for I am with you; do not be dismayed, for I am your God. I will strengthen you...' (Isaiah 41:10). And the note that accompanied this verse could have been written with this person in mind. She was able to face the day knowing she was safe in God's hands. Now, some people will call that a happy coincidence—but was it? It is through the words of the Bible that God speaks to us—either by our 'just happening' to read an appropriate verse at the right time, or by bringing the right words into our minds because we are already familiar with them. What an amazing resource we have as we look ahead to the new millennium!

Future hope…
As 1999 draws to a close and we begin to wonder what will happen to us and to our world in the next millennium, our writers have looked for verses that will inspire and encourage. Elaine Pountney reminds us that we have the gift of peace from Jesus that 'transforms us right in the middle of our very real lives', and that 'in our out-of-control world God has plans for you… plans to give you hope and a future'. Then Margaret Killingray takes us through passages from Isaiah and Revelation where we are 'given a vision, a picture of the future, a promise that one day we will know all the answers, that we will discover what our lives were for'. I will leave you to read for yourself each day words that will inspire you and assure you that nothing is random in God's plan for you and for me.

As we live out the last days of this millennium and as we prepare to celebrate the 2000th year of the birth of Christ, my trust is that we will grow even more secure in the knowledge that whatever lies ahead, God is with us. Hallelujah!

Mary Reid

Contributors

Beryl Adamsbaum is a language teacher living in France, just across the border from Geneva, Switzerland, where she and her husband have been engaged in Christian ministry for thirty years. She is involved in teaching, preaching and counselling. She is the editor of her church magazine and writes short devotional articles.

Diana Archer has three young children and a degree in religious studies, and has served in Japan as a missionary. She has worked in the publishing world as a freelance editor and writer. Her book *Who'd Plant a Church?* has been highly acclaimed.

Rosemary Green has an international speaking ministry, sometimes alongside her husband Michael. Her highly praised book *God's Catalyst* distils her wisdom and experience gained through many years of prayer counselling. She is on the pastoral staff of Wycliffe Theological College in Oxford.

Margaret Killingray is a tutor at the Institute for Contemporary Christianity in London. She has assisted Dr John Stott and others in running Christian Impact conferences here and overseas, and is the author of *The Way to Live* (see the Magazine section for an extract from this new book). Margaret and her husband, David, have three daughters and four grandchildren.

Jennifer Rees Larcombe, one of Britain's best-loved Christian authors and speakers, lives in Kent. She looks at messages given to us from the Christmas narrative that will help us look agead to the new millennium. In recent years she has published a novel, the *Children's Bible Story Book*, and an account of her dramatic recovery, *Unexpected Healing*.

Christine Leonard lives in Surrey with her husband and two teenage children. She writes books for both adults and children; most tell the true stories of ordinary Christians who have done extraordinary things. She is the Vice-President of the Association of Christian Writers.

Bridget Plass studied at drama school and is a sought-after speaker who, when family commitments permit, often travels with her husband Adrian. Her book *The Apple of His Eye* made its way into the top twenty Christian titles in 1997. But life, as she confesses, is not always lived at the top.

Elaine Pountney is a dynamic conference and retreat speaker, presently working as a management consultant in the corporate world. She is married to Michael, an Anglican priest, and has two married daughters, one in England and one on Vancouver Island. Elaine enjoys playing tennis and knitting Aran sweaters for her grandchild.

Christina Rees was born in America and came to live in England twenty years ago when she met and married Chris Rees. She is a freelance writer and broadcaster, speaker, preacher and a member of the General Synod of the Church of England and the Archbishops' Council. She is also Chair of WATCH (Women and the Church), a national organization that provides a forum for promoting women in the Church.

Alie Stibbe has contributed to *Renewal* and other Christian publications. She lives at St Andrew's Vicarage, Chorleywood, where her husband Mark is the vicar. Previously they ministered in Sheffield. They have four children; the youngest is three years old.

Contributors are identified by their initials at the bottom of each page.

A Morning Prayer

Thank you, heavenly Father,
for this new day.
Be with me now
in all I do
and think
and say,
that it will be to your glory.

Amen

What is prayer?

So give yourselves humbly to God. Resist the devil and he will flee from you. And when you draw close to God, God will draw close to you. Wash your hands you sinners, and let your hearts be filled with God alone to make them pure and true to him.

Many people have written about prayer and its dynamics over the centuries, but for me, prayer is simply our drawing near to God in order that he can draw near to us. Finding ways to enter and stay in God's presence is something I have covered in a previous set of readings, as is humility, the attribute we need in order to desire to be in God's presence at all. Prayer is what happens when you are in God's presence, and is an umbrella term that covers a multitude of manners of communication.

There are a lot of people in the Church who are giants of prayer. One can feel very daunted by such commitment and think that it is not worth trying at all because one hasn't got the time or the energy to devote in the same way as they do. You would be right to think that you might not be able to pray in the same way, but wrong to think it is not worth starting at all. For the busy parent, daily intercession may not be on the agenda, but God is happy to be acknowledged in many other ways in keeping with your situation.

Often, all there is time and energy for is a sigh as you sit on the side of the bed in the morning, that breathes in the Spirit and whispers, 'I desire you, Lord, and to do your will. Strengthen me.' You can be sure that God draws near and honours it.

The purpose of prayer is to invite God to live inside us, so our greatest desire is always to obey his will. The mind thus becomes the temple of God, and the soul becomes his friend.
BASIL (C. 330–379)

AHS

11

The Lord, my comfort

Now let your lovingkindness comfort me, just as you promised. Surround me with your tender mercies, that I may live. For your law is my delight. Help me to love your every wish; then I will never have to be ashamed of myself. I faint for your salvation; but I expect your help, for you have promised it.

When we are busy and stressed, it may be a long time before we realize that we haven't stopped for more than an early morning sigh of prayer and really spent time with God. It is the same when you realize that life has become so hectic that you and your loved one have not sat down and given each other a chance to have a really good talk. It can sometimes be difficult to know where to begin. Often the best thing to do is to rest in each other's company, drawing reassurance from each other until the moment to talk arrives.

It can be the same with us and the Lord. He is always with us, but if we haven't really spoken to him for a while, we can think that God won't want to hear from us. Actually, he is like the father of the prodigal son, waiting with arms open wide to embrace us as soon as we make the steps towards them. Then we receive what we so desperately need: to be wrapped in his reassuring embrace until we regain confidence in our relationship and can talk again.

Grab that twenty minutes that presents itself, find a quiet and secure place to sit, and say, 'Here I am, Lord; enfold me.' Rest and then eventually let the talking begin.

I saw that he is to us everything that is good and comfortable for us. He is our clothing which for love enwraps us, holds us, and all encloses us because of his tender love, so that he may never leave us.
JULIAN OF NORWICH

AHS

Letting it all out

Lord, I am not proud and haughty. I don't think myself better than others. I don't pretend to 'know it all'. I am quiet now before the Lord, just as a child who is weaned from the breast. Yes, my begging has been stilled. O Israel, you too should quietly trust in the Lord—now, and always.

I was sent a card recently with this verse on it. The picture on the front was of a small baby asleep on its mother's shoulder. The baby may have been asleep, but it was not old enough to be weaned and was going to wake up and become angry and demanding again. It would be months before the baby would be old enough to sit on its mother's knee without rummaging!

Yesterday I suggested sitting quietly wrapped up in the Lord's love. However, like the baby, there is only going to be a certain length of time we can sit like that before we start rummaging and allow all the unresolved conflict inside to start rising up to the surface.

It is a valid form of prayer to let all this flotsam wash up before God in a storm of emotion. The psalmists did it all the time. You actually have to be quite secure in the love of the person you are speaking to in order to let it all out this way! God loves us so much, I am sure he would rather have all the junk out than in. Once we have poured out our anguish and are ready to receive, the Lord can start pouring his comfort into those sore places. God is like the mother in this psalm: one of the Old Testament names for God is El Shaddai, and one of its connotations is 'the God who breastfeeds'! Once we have calmed down enough to receive, there is more than enough to satisfy.

Lord, I have a lot of catching up to do with you; just let me pour it all out before you today and then satisfy me with your comfort. Amen
AHS

Lord, teach me to pray

Once when Jesus had been out praying, one of his disciples came to him as he finished and said, 'Lord, teach us a prayer to recite just as John [the Baptist] taught one to his disciples.'

I am hoping that the last few days' readings will have got you to a place where you have (re-)established contact and are ready to learn to pray! Starting to learn a new skill can be quite tedious, as there can be so much preamble before you get going. I have recently started to learn a new language (Norwegian!) and because I have no one to help me with the unfamiliar pronunciations, I have often had to turn back to the beginning to make sure I am doing it right. Then we had some visitors from Norway and I found the courage to sit and read to one of them. At first I was afraid of making a fool of myself, but she was so encouraging that soon I found my confidence growing and was willing to tackle something more difficult.

Learning to talk to God can seem like learning a foreign language too. Thankfully, the Lord understands us and all we need to do is screw up our courage and talk to him. In today's passage Jesus shows us the basic framework for prayer. If we follow it, we soon realize that we know quite a lot already and gain confidence to try something harder.

The Lord's Prayer can be split into several sections:

- Worshipping God for who he is.
- Asking that God will have his way in our lives and the world.
- Asking for our practical needs.
- Asking for forgiveness and forgiving others.
- Asking for his help in the difficulties of life.
- Acknowledging his power and Lordship.

Take time to pray the Lord's Prayer, thinking about what each phrase means. Then write out your own version, expressing your thoughts, even if it takes a lot of paper!

AHS

The secret place

But when you pray, go away by yourself, all alone, and shut the door behind you and pray to your Father secretly, and your Father, who knows your secrets, will reward you.

I used to find it impossible to have time to be alone when I had four children, a husband and five animals in the house, and the parish on the phone and the doorstep, so I learned to 'pray on the hoof' and this taught me many valuable lessons. Perhaps I am forgetting too quickly the joys and exhaustion of caring for new babies and toddlers, when even the quiet space of a night feed leaves us too exhausted to do more than fling our unspoken emotions towards heaven. But I have returned to the realization that God needs our regular, undivided attention, as well as our continuous attentiveness.

There really is no getting round it. Jesus says, 'When you pray', not 'If you pray'. For me, this has become a real challenge. If I have the motivation to learn a new language and take up the flute, both needing significant practice that requires time and space, then I have no excuse not to find a time and place to give God my undivided attention in prayer.

When I was away at school there was no privacy at all; at one point I was sharing a room with ten other girls. As a young Christian I was determined to find somewhere quiet to read the Bible and pray. My favourite place was on the fire-escape steps in the laundry room, shielded from sight by a stack of laundry hampers. When that became impossible, I used to lock myself in one of the sixth-form bathrooms before breakfast. During those times in the secret place, the Lord taught me many things that saw me through the difficult times that I was unaware lay ahead.

Lord, challenge my heart and my schedule to make the time and to seek out a secret place in which I can give you my full attention every day. Amen

AHS

Distracted by many things

*She came to Jesus and said, 'Sir, doesn't it seem unfair to you
that my sister just sits here while I do all the work? Tell her to
come and help me.' But the Lord said to her, 'Martha, dear
friend, you are so upset over all these details! There is really
only one thing worth being concerned about. Mary has
discovered it—and I won't take it away from her!'*

I am a very organized and tidy person, and I find it difficult to sit
down and spend time on myself unless the house is shipshape. I
have had to learn that to make time for God I have to make a
conscious effort to ignore all the things that need doing and to
simplify my lifestyle and environment so that it requires minimal
maintenance.

This is what I had to do to fit in my new hobbies. I then felt
very challenged. If I was willing to rearrange my life to accommodate these desires, I should be just as willing to rearrange
things to accommodate time with God. Yesterday morning I
decided to do just that. I asked the Lord to wake me up early. I
reorganized the morning routine to allow myself half an hour for
prayer and a devotional reading. I was amazed how straightforward it was and how much better I felt for it. All the distractions
of the day fell into place in such a way that I was running an
hour ahead of schedule all day!

As Jesus said to Martha, there is really only one thing worth
being concerned about. If we spend time at the Lord's feet, the
rest of our problems and needs will fall into their proper perspective.

*Lord, forgive me for the times that I have not given you the attention
you long for and deserve. Forgive me for allowing my perspectives to
become distorted. Help me to reorder my life so that you have the
prime place in my affections so that other concerns fall into their proper place. Amen*

AHS

Making every moment count

Let the peace of heart which comes from Christ be always present in your hearts and lives, for this is your responsibility and privilege as members of his body. And always be thankful... And whatever you do or say, let it be as a representative of the Lord Jesus Christ, and come with him into the presence of God the Father to give him your thanks.

When we have spent time in prayer, it can be very easy to pack God up in a little box and carry on regardless until the next time we stop and pray. A real challenge of prayer is to be able to take the presence of God that we found in our devotional time out into the rest of the day with us. Most of us lead very ordinary lives and are not in what might obviously be termed 'full-time ministry'. However, even in life's mundane routines we can turn each moment into a living, breathing prayer by doing 'every thing as unto the Lord'.

In order to practise this, it can be helpful to slow life down. We are all so rushed that we often miss the presence of God in the ordinary things around us. The next thing to do is to allow the Holy Spirit to prompt your heart while you are performing a particular chore. When I am tying the children's shoelaces, I think of Jesus washing the disciples' feet. I pray for humility and use the opportunity of the physical contact to bless the children as they go out into the day. When I am vacuuming, I think of the woman and the lost coin and pray for the lost.

O God, deliver me from my distractions, which are many, and lead me to a quiet place of devotion at your feet. Teach me there how to pause... help me see something. So much passes me by without attention, let alone appreciation; without reflection, let alone reverence; without thought, let alone thankfulness. Slow me down, Lord.
KEN GIRE, WINDOWS OF THE SOUL, ZONDERVAN

AHS

Presenting requests

Always be full of joy in the Lord; I say it again, rejoice! ...
Don't worry about anything; instead pray about everything;
tell God your needs and don't forget to thank him for his
answers. If you do this you will experience God's peace, which
is far more wonderful than the human mind can understand.

I often feel guilty about coming before the Lord and asking him for anything because I spent a lot of my younger life having to be self-sufficient. I also find it hard to come straight out and ask God for anything because a lot of emphasis is often put on not approaching God with a mile-long list! I think that the latter viewpoint has been frequently put in order to help people learn about other dimensions of prayer. However, this does not mean we should not ask the Lord for our needs. He knows there are things we need and he loves to provide them (Matthew 6:8).

I often find I am so burdened by something that we lack materially that I rush into the Lord's presence and come straight out with it, feeling guilty that I haven't spent adequate time in worship or confession first. It's rather like my children rushing in from school saying they need a specific thing for a task ahead. Once they have the assurance that all will be provided, there is time for other chat! It was like that this morning—I had to pray about the shopping I'd done on a visit to Sweden. How was I going to pay for it? Later the post arrived. In it was a birthday card from an aunt containing a generous cheque! I rushed off to the bank, thanking the Lord profusely.

Lord, thank you that you are interested in the smallest needs and problems that we have, that we have no worries about presenting them before you. Now I want to spend time telling you all those things that are weighing me down. I ask you to provide what I need and point out what is unnecessary. Amen

AHS

Living in fellowship with Christ

If we say we are his friends, but go on living in spiritual darkness and sin, we are lying. But if we are living in the light of God's presence, just as Christ does, then we have wonderful fellowship and joy with each other, and the blood of Jesus his Son cleanses us from every sin... [But] if we confess our sins to him, he can be depended upon to forgive us and to cleanse us from every wrong.

There are times when we don't want to talk to the Lord in prayer. This is usually because we feel we have been wronged or that we have done something wrong ourselves. The longer it gets left, the worse it becomes, until we end up not knowing why we stopped talking, and being too embarrassed to put it right.

In the children's prayer of confession at our church, we admit our sins so that we can be 'together with God without it feeling difficult'. There is no point in hiding anything from a God who knows our innermost thoughts anyway! To stay in fellowship with the Father we need to live a life that cultivates personal confession as an attribute, if not a discipline.

Confession is not quite the same as saying 'sorry'. Confession is actually agreeing with the Lord that the thing we have thought, said or done is wrong. When we do this, repentance (sorry) comes a lot more easily. Sometimes we need someone else's help with confession. When we doubt that Christ has dealt with the issue, the person who has helped us can remind us that the matter is forgotten. Confession is central to maintaining a healthy prayer life—neglect it at your risk!

Although it pains me to repeat it, yet for truth's sake I will accuse myself, that I may better deserve your mercy. Guilty and confused, what shall I say? I can but say, 'I have sinned, O Lord, I have sinned; be merciful and forgive.'

THOMAS À KEMPIS, THE IMITATION OF CHRIST

AHS

Praying with others

Jesus said, 'And I tell you this—if two of you agree down here on earth concerning anything you ask for, my Father in heaven will do it for you. For where two or three gather together because they are mine, I will be there among them.'

After beginning the adventure in prayer alone, it is natural to want to get together with others to share the burden of a concern and the excitement of seeing God answer. Jesus promises that when we meet together like this, our praying becomes more effective for God's kingdom. This is 'intercession' and basically means that we are committed together to 'stand in the gap' and seek the Lord concerning a particular situation.

This sort of prayer is the spiritual foundation of many churches and ministries, which, without this undergirding, would not be half as effective for the Lord. Although intercession is a special ministry, the Lord chooses ordinary people like you and me to undertake it. If we are humble and willing to accept the challenge, over a period of time, we will become like the prayer warriors whom we so often admire from afar.

It may be difficult when we first join a prayer group. I am extremely shy in such situations. However, we cannot hide behind our shyness or fear of ridicule for ever. Sometimes the Holy Spirit lays such a burden upon our hearts to pray for a particular person or situation that we know we are going to burn up if we don't speak it out. What we need to remember is that the other people in the group are there to pray, not to wait and see what a fool you might make of yourself!

There are believers who can teach us much by praying with them. Praying regularly with others can be one of the most enriching experiences of your Christian life… When you make something a priority, you will sacrifice for it, give time to it.
DONALD S. WHITNEY, SPIRITUAL DISCIPLINES FOR THE CHRISTIAN LIFE, SCRIPTURE PRESS

AHS

Praying in the Spirit

By our faith, the Holy Spirit helps us with our daily problems and in our praying. For we don't even know what we should pray for, nor how to pray as we should; but the Holy Spirit prays for us with such feeling that it cannot be expressed in words. And the Father who knows all hearts knows, of course, what the Spirit is saying as he pleads for us in harmony with God's own will.

There is much more to say about prayer, but I would like to end this section by mentioning 'praying in the Spirit'.

When we give our lives to Christ, the Holy Spirit comes and lives within us (v. 9), and it is the same 'Holy Spirit that speaks to us deep in our hearts, and tells us that we really are God's children' (v. 16). The Holy Spirit helps us with our praying. When we don't know how to pray about a disturbing situation, such as a terrible natural disaster, we can feel a deep sighing inside us. This is the Holy Spirit within us aligning our desire to pray for the situation with God's desire and purpose. Of course we cannot know what God would ultimately want in such circumstances, but the Holy Spirit 'translates' what we are longing to say into words that God is longing to hear. Praying in the Spirit is like a slow-play videotape put on at normal speed: we cannot understand it. But God, who, metaphorically, has the 'right equipment', can understand it perfectly.

Sometimes, people praying in the Spirit can do nothing but cry; others pray quietly, using the gift of tongues. God hears and understands. It must be made clear that praying in the Spirit is not the same as the use of a 'spirit guide' or astral projection. These things must be avoided at all costs (Leviticus 19:26b, 31).

Make Ephesians 3:14–21 your prayer for today.

AHS

Truth or tradition?

And as they were speaking to the people, the priests and the captain of the temple and the Sadducees came upon them, annoyed because they were teaching the people and proclaiming in Jesus the resurrection from the dead.

The book of Acts begins with the dramatic outpouring of the Holy Spirit upon the disciples gathered in the upper room. Then there are the wonderful stories of Peter preaching, of how the early Christians lived together in a communal way, and of how Peter and John healed a lame man. At the beginning of chapter 4, the problems begin.

Everything was going brilliantly, with thousands of people being baptized, and an atmosphere of praise and thanksgiving surrounding the group of believers. Then came the persecution.

The saddest thing of all is that the problems were started by the religious authorities, just as with Jesus. The people who were listening were hungry for the message that the disciples preached and were eager to hear about Jesus, but the custodians of orthodoxy could not tolerate any deviation from their own teaching.

I have often wondered whether I would have been won over by the fire and passion of the Spirit-inspired disciples, or whether I would have shrunk back from their message of the Messiah who had come and conquered death, and who now offered all people the hope of eternal life.

For those of us raised in a Christian family and familiar with the concepts of the Christian faith, it is difficult to imagine what it must have been like for those staunch Jewish establishment figures, or what it is like for people today who know nothing of the gospel of Christ. When we tell others about Jesus, we need to take great care in how we present what we believe to be the truth. We need to sit lightly to the traditions of our faith that have little to do with the core message of the good news of Jesus Christ.

Living Lord, help me to love your truth more than human-made traditions. Amen
Read Isaiah 55:8–9.

CR

Nothing stops the Holy Spirit!

And they arrested them and put them in custody until the morrow, for it was already evening. But many of those who heard the word believed; and the number of those came to about five thousand.

There is something almost comical about the irritated and threatened religious authorities who thought they could put an end to the spread of Christianity by throwing Peter and John in prison. Clearly, they had left it too late! As a result of the apostles' preaching to the crowds, another five thousand people believed in Jesus as the Christ.

It's as if the priests and other religious élite were trying to put the lid back onto a pot that was bubbling over, and, of course, that doesn't work. The only way to stop a pot from boiling over is to remove it from the source of heat. Peter and John couldn't be removed from their source of 'heat', because they had the Holy Spirit inside of them. Wherever they went, they took the Spirit with them.

That is the same today for anyone who has said 'yes' to Jesus, said sorry for their sins, and opened their hearts to God. God has promised that the Holy Spirit will come and live inside them, and fill them with the same power and love that filled the early disciples to overflowing.

If you feel you're lacking something in your life of faith, ask God to open up your heart more to the Holy Spirit. And then trust. God *wants* to fill your entire being with the light and love of his Spirit. And when you're full, you'll start to bubble over. You will probably not even be aware of it, but others will be blessed just by being around you.

Lord of power and love, please make us hungry for more of you, so that we might be filled to overflowing, for Jesus' sake. Amen
Read Ephesians 3:14–21.

CR

By what power do you live?

Be it known to you all, and to all the people of Israel, that by the name of Jesus Christ of Nazareth, whom you crucified, whom God raised from the dead, by him this man is standing before you well.

Peter and John had spent the night in prison. That alone would be enough to unsettle most of us. The next morning they were taken into a room filled with potentially intimidating people—elders, rulers, scribes and all the high priests. These men were as serious and long-faced a bunch of people as you could imagine.

They had gathered for one reason: to ask Peter and John a question. They wanted to know in what power or name the disciples had healed the lame man. They were not accusing the disciples of lying or of only pretending to have healed the man. They just wanted to know by what power they were operating.

Ever since the coming of the Holy Spirit at Pentecost, Peter had been a changed man. The old Peter, who had denied even knowing Jesus and who ran away when Jesus was crucified, was dead and gone. A new Peter, bold and fearless, now stood before these educated, powerful, yet anxious men.

In a few words, Peter outlined who Jesus was, what his life signified, and how they, too, might be saved. Peter gave all the credit to Jesus, and emphasized that Jesus was the Christ, the one sent by God to save the people of Israel.

Where before Peter had been impulsive, now he was incisive; where he had been weak, now he was strong; where he had been crushed, now he was confident. No wonder that those who had known the old Peter were so keen to discover the secret of how and why he had become such a different person.

Dear God of transformations, please help us to believe we can change, and help us to trust you to do the changing. Amen
Read John 19:15–27.

                                                          CR

Who is Jesus to you?

And there is salvation in no one else, for there is no other name under heaven given among men by which we must be saved.

We're all supposed to know that Jesus saves, but what does it really mean? A few years after I had an experience of being completely drenched and infused with God's love, I had another unforgettable experience. It was the middle of the night and I was asleep on my bed, which was just a mattress on the floor. I began to realize that I was sobbing for joy with the love I felt for Jesus.

At first I thought it was a dream, but then I became aware of the room around me and of the reality of my tears. I turned over and propped myself up on my elbows. I felt very strongly that Jesus was standing right in front of me. I was aware of his feet close to my head. He stood there for a while, and I continued to sob, now with joy as well as love. Then he said to me, 'I am your friend, I am your Saviour, I am your king.' Then Jesus left and I was alone in the room again.

Afterwards, I felt as if I had met with Jesus. I have thought about his words for many years, and they continue to give me strength, comfort and purpose.

Many of us live our lives at such a fast pace, going from one activity to the next, with barely a pause between. From time to time, the memory of that night arrests me when I am in the middle of a busy day, and for a moment there is stillness, and once again I am alone with my Lord, who is, in a way I will never be able to describe adequately, my friend, my Saviour and my king.

Dear Lord, thank you for loving us and for being our Saviour, even if we don't yet know what that really means. Amen
Read 1 John 3:1–2.

CR

Who do you spend time with?

Now when they saw the boldness of Peter and John, and
perceived that they were uneducated, common men, they
wondered; and they recognized that they had been with Jesus.

The implications of this verse are unmistakable. The religious
authorities knew that Peter and John, on their own, would not
have been able to speak as they did. Not only did their words
impress these men, but their attitude and character as well. Here
were two supposedly simple men, who spoke with unnatural clarity, perception and authority. The religious officials come to an
inevitable conclusion: these men had been with Jesus.

What was it about Jesus that had so evidently rubbed off on
Peter and John? Was it that they were not afraid to answer the
questions put to them? Certainly, Jesus had never shirked from
responding to questions, even the ones asked in order to catch
him out. Was it that Peter and John seemed to know more than
they should have, given their education and upbringing? Clearly,
they had got their teaching and insights from somewhere.

Or was it that Peter and John possessed an inner strength and
calm that seemed so at odds with their circumstances and situation. They should have been frightened, unsure, daunted, but
here they were, at peace and unfazed by their inquisitors.

I believe that it is possible for us today to become like the
emboldened and quietly confident Peter and John. To do so, we
need to spend time with Jesus in prayer and allow ourselves to be
filled with the Holy Spirit.

Lord Jesus, we want people to look at us and know that we have been
with you. Please fill us with the Holy Spirit so that we might carry on
the work of spreading your truth and light in the world around us.
Amen
Read Matthew 7:7–8.

                                                              CR

You can't argue with experience

What shall we do with these men? For that a notable sign has been performed through them is manifest to all the inhabitants of Jerusalem, and we cannot deny it.

This verse holds a key for anyone wishing to persuade anyone else of the truth of Christianity: actions speak louder than words. If Peter and John's confident words had not been accompanied by the reality of the healed man, the discussion with the priests and elders could have been held on an academic, intellectual plane. 'Jesus is the Christ' … 'No he isn't' … 'Yes he is' … and so on.

The presence of the formerly lame man was a reality that these men could not deny. They had seen him for years, huddled on the ground, unable to walk, and now here he was, standing before them, perfectly well. They couldn't argue with his experience.

Many of us get hung up on living a 'correct' Christian life, and, depending on our own particular Christian community, we jump through all sorts of hoops that have little to do with living a life of faith in response to what almighty God has done for us. We take such care to present the right image to our fellow Christians and to unbelievers (if we ever bump into any of those) that we fail to notice that we're actually holding up masks that increasingly disguise who we really are.

In order for us to show others what God has done for us, we first have to show them that we're not already perfect to start with. I was lame, but now I can walk. I was blind, but now I can see. What has Jesus done for you?

Dear God of power and might, help us to acknowledge our weaknesses and needs, so that when you heal us, we might be able to tell others what you have done for us. Amen
Read Matthew 9:10–13.

CR

What is your authority?

But Peter and John answered them, 'Whether it is right in the sight of God to listen to you rather than to God, you must judge; for we cannot but speak of what we have seen and heard.'

Some of us are naturally rebellious, some of us are naturally obedient. Most of us are a combination of the two. For some, going along with what we're taught in church is a comfortable, obvious path; for others, being told things is a sign to start questioning.

I live with a natural questioner. He must have been an exhausting child! I was more of a natural sponge, soaking up the teaching I received. It wasn't until what I had been taught created such a dissonance with my reality that I started to examine things in a more objective way. It was only after a particularly difficult time that I began to ask more penetrating and searching questions about my faith.

With the help of the Bible and other books, and by talking with a few Christian friends (including my naturally rigorous husband!), I began to find a way forward through my difficulties. My understanding of God changed. My understanding of myself changed. I had to discard some of what I had been taught in the past, and some of my pet beliefs about God, myself and others. It was liberating—and scary.

If the religious authorities had only been able to accept what Peter was saying to them, they too could have become disciples of the living Lord. Instead, they did not allow themselves to be swayed by the truth right in front of their eyes—because it clashed with what they had been taught in the past. Their preconceived notions of who the Messiah would be prevented them from recognizing Jesus as the Christ.

Lord, no matter what happens to us, help us always to be able to see you.
Read Matthew 16:13–20.

                                                                      CR

Meeting each other's needs

There was not a needy person among them, for as many as were possessors of lands or houses sold them, and brought the proceeds of what was sold and laid it at the apostles' feet; and distribution was made to each as any had need.

So many of us have been taught to look to Jesus to have our needs met. We pray, usually without telling anyone else how desperate we are, and then we wait. I have heard amazing and inspiring stories of people who needed money in order to do something absolutely vital, receiving anonymous envelopes filled with cash, or of relative strangers responding to their needs out of the blue.

Yet, in the earliest Church, the apostles took responsibility for those who believed. Those in the community of the faithful who had valuable possessions, sold them and gave the proceeds to the apostles, who then made sure that everyone had enough. Can you imagine our churches operating like that now!

We as churches and individuals give generously to charities, and we may also give in private to the special needs we see around us, but no longer do the leaders of our churches take public responsibility for the local Christian community in quite the same way as the apostles did.

Whether or not that is the ideal we should aim for, I believe the principle is still the same: we are to meet each other's needs. We have been given the Holy Spirit, who can give us discernment and wisdom. We have been told to practise hospitality, and to be generous. Above all, we should be forming the heart and mind of Christ, which will make us just, merciful and full of compassion.

Dear Lord, make me aware of those who are in need around me, and show me how to help them. Please help others to see my needs and meet them, knowing that all things come from you. Amen
Read 1 Corinthians 13.

CR

Cheating God

But a man named Ananias with his wife Sapphira sold a piece of property, and with his wife's knowledge he kept back some of the proceeds, and brought only a part and laid it at the apostles' feet.

No one had asked this couple to sell their land. It was their own decision, and they were free to give the money to whomever they chose, or to keep it for themselves. In the event, they sold it, and gave a portion of the proceeds to the church. Nothing wrong with that, in fact, on the surface, it was an act of generosity. But in their hearts they were cheating God.

This disturbing passage shows starkly how it is the intentions of our hearts that count. It also shows that Ananias and Sapphira did not give from the heart, but rather from a grudging sense of duty. They resented parting with their money, and it is clear that they also thought that the apostles (and God) would have demanded that they give everything.

But Peter was not fooled. He discerned what Ananias had done and told him how wrong, and pointless, his actions were—whereupon Ananias promptly fell down dead, followed shortly by his wife.

What we do is important, and the more good deeds we do, the better, but *why* we do something is crucial. We need to be honest with ourselves and with God, and ask the Holy Spirit to fine tune our consciences so that we will act only out of genuine love, truth and mercy. The beauty of what Christ does through us is that he takes our faltering, but genuine, decisions made in his name, and uses them to bless people out of all proportion to what we have done.

Lord, whose will it is to give us abundant life, help us to respond to your love so that when we give to others we do so with honest and loving hearts. Amen
Read Matthew 6:1–4.

CR

A healing touch

*And more than ever believers were added to the Lord,
multitudes both of men and women, so that they carried out
the sick into the streets, and laid them on beds and pallets,
that as Peter came by at least his shadow might fall on some
of them.*

One of the most frequent comments about the late Princess
Diana is that wherever she went, people who met her felt better.
It is said that her mere presence in a hospital ward would bring
fresh joy and hope to the patients and to the staff. For some people, meeting Diana was a turning point in their lives, and they
went on to face their challenges with greater courage and peace.

What was it that Princess Diana was spreading? What was
the secret of her touch? I believe it was identification and compassion. She could feel the pain of other people in an unusually
deep way, and she was filled to overflowing with compassion for
them. Sadly, I do not know whether Diana ever learned where
all her loving instincts and her desire to reach out to others came
from. If only she had been able to give the credit and glory to
Jesus, what an amazing witness she would have been. As it was,
her life, like all of ours, was patchy, but people were focused on
her as a person, and not on the one who gave her such great love
for others.

In contrast, Peter and the other apostles performed healings
and miracles, and they gave all the credit to Jesus Christ.
Evidently, Peter was so filled with the Holy Spirit that even his
shadow brought healing to the sick. I wonder what effect *my*
presence has on the people around me?

*Dear Lord, help us to be so close to you that wherever we go we
spread your loving, healing touch. Amen*
Read John 14:12–17.

                                                              CR

In the centre of God's will

But the high priest rose up and all who were with him, that is, the party of the Sadducees, and filled with jealousy they arrested the apostles and put them in the common prison.

The last time the high priests threw Peter and the other apostles into prison, it backfired spectacularly! The moment the apostles got home, they started praying and asking God for increased strength and courage, and 'the place in which they were gathered together was shaken; they were all filled with the Holy Spirit and spoke the word of God with boldness' (Acts 4:31).

So much for prison and threats putting an end to the apostles' preaching, teaching and healing! Peter was not trying to cause trouble, but neither was he prepared to stop doing what he knew God wanted him to do. The choice was straightforward: either obey the earthly authorities or obey God.

Some negative reactions in our lives we bring on ourselves, by being insensitive, obtuse or pig-headed. Some unwelcome reactions are a result of our being obedient to God. One of the greatest challenges of the Christian walk is to learn obedience, and then to learn when it is our obedience that is causing people problems, and when our own stubborn natures.

The apostles were so confident that they were doing exactly what they were meant to be doing that imprisonment and opposition just made them stronger and bolder. The only way we can have that same type of confidence is if we keep so close to Jesus, so filled with the Holy Spirit, that we experience God's presence and the peace that passes understanding. Even then, I can't imagine ever feeling sanguine about being thrown into prison!

Dear Lord, please spare us persecution for our faith, but if it comes, fill us with your strength and peace. We pray for those who are in prison or being tortured because of their loyalty to you. Amen
Read Isaiah 26:3.

CR

Gamaliel's advice

But a Pharisee in the council named Gamaliel, a teacher of the law, held in honour by all the people, stood up and ordered the men to be put outside for a while. And he said to them, 'Men of Israel, take care what you do with these men.'

Thank God for a God-fearing lawyer like Gamaliel! He came to the apostles' defence in an unusual way, by citing the precedent of two other cases where strong leaders had persuaded hundreds of men to follow them, but where their efforts ended in disaster.

Gamaliel convinced the religious authorities that if the apostles were acting in their own strength, their actions would fail, but if they were acting in God's name, they would be invincible. Gamaliel was even worried that by opposing the apostles, should it transpire that they were indeed obeying God, the religious authorities would find themselves in the dreadful position of opposing God! This logic swayed the high priests and they let the apostles go, ordering them not to speak in the name of Jesus.

Even today, the 'Gamaliel principle', as it is known, is used in response to everything from major church decisions to private individual matters. It is a particularly prudent way forward when it is difficult to see whether something is of God or not. Of course there are times and situations when it is important to react immediately, but there are also times when the wisest course of action is to wait and see whether or not God is at work.

Lord, let us trust you enough to allow you to work in the lives of people and situations. Give us wisdom and a love of your truth. Amen

CR

Are we willing to suffer?

Then they left the presence of the council, rejoicing that they were counted worthy to suffer dishonour for the name.

I don't know about you, but my own response to suffering, even for the sake of the gospel, isn't usually to rejoice! In fact, I can remember some painful times at secondary school, where I was one of very few Christians. Standing up for Christ was most decidedly uncool. Once I stuck up for a younger student who was being bullied, and I was made to feel like a spoilsport. Of course, I gained one grateful new friend!

At other times, I found it desperately lonely and difficult to keep to the moral standards I believed I was called to follow. Most of the men who were attracted to me, and vice versa, were not fellow Christians. They didn't understand me, and few bothered to find out about my faith.

Even though I say I have suffered, it is nothing compared to what so many Christians have had to endure. When I read the lives of the martyrs, I always feel humbled and grateful: humbled by their courage and fortitude, and grateful that I have not had to go through the same horrific experiences.

Just recently, I was asked if I could offer hospitality for a couple of days to a man who was going through a crisis in his life. I gladly agreed, but was instantly rattled when I heard he would be bringing his three-year-old son. I am ashamed to say that my first thought was to worry about whether the child would destroy my house. As it happened, the little boy was adorable and perfectly well behaved, and we had a wonderful time together. I just regret that my first thoughts about him were centred on my own peace and comfort.

Dear Lord, you went through pain, suffering and death for us. Please help us to be willing to follow you, even if it means we have to suffer. Amen
Read Isaiah 53.

                                                              CR

And where is our enthusiasm?

And every day in the temple and at home they did not cease teaching and preaching Jesus as the Christ.

If I had to go to church every day, and attend a Bible study every night, I think I would run a mile! All right, I love going to some churches, and I love to lead worship and preach. I also like to read the Bible, in my own time, by myself, but the thought of all that corporate worship brings out the dormant hermit in me.

Undoubtedly, part of the problem is the way some services are conducted. The leaders are stilted, and there is no expectation of joy. Pettiness and correctness, rather than praise and wonder, dominate the atmosphere. I sometimes imagine that if one of the early Christians, or even Jesus himself, were to wander into such a service they would not recognize what was supposed to be going on!

Another part of the problem lies with the people in the pews. If they insist upon keeping things a certain way, because that's the way it's always been done, then any new vicar with bright ideas is in for a rough time.

We need to concentrate on our own spiritual lives, and to reach out to others around us who may not know how to grow close to God. We also need to bring our whole selves into church, and refuse to play the game of 'let's pretend': let's pretend that everything is OK, or let's pretend that I'm above most other mortals. Let's *not* pretend, but try to be open and honest and show real care and compassion for each other. The churches I have gone to that have been like that have truly been a taste of heaven.

Dear Lord, forgive us for being lukewarm and for not putting you first when we come together to worship you. Please rekindle our sense of wonder and awe in your presence. Amen
Read 1 Thessalonians 5:16–24.

CR

Cloud of witnesses

Since we are surrounded by so great a cloud of witnesses, let us also lay aside every weight and the sin that clings so closely, and let us run with perseverance the race that is set before us, looking to Jesus.

It is not surprising that Dorothy L. Sayers, writer of detective novels and well versed in the scriptures, chose the above title (slightly modified to *Clouds of Witnesses*) when relating Lord Peter Wimsey's defence of his brother, falsely accused of murder!

However, our passage today is nothing to do with a murder trial; it is nothing to do with death at all. On the contrary, it tells us how to live! It exhorts us to take courage from those believers who have gone before, mentioned in the previous chapter. With this mighty 'cloud of witnesses' cheering us on, we are to run the race, with no distractions, keeping our eyes on the finishing line, where the one who ran the race before us is waiting.

Now, I play tennis. And I know that if I want to win, I need to keep my eye on the ball and concentrate fully on the game. No distracting thoughts. No gazing at the scenery. What kind of distractions could cause us to falter in the race? This passage mentions two: 'every weight' and 'the sin that clings so closely'. 'Every weight' could be anything that holds us back in our Christian life. Sometimes we need to choose between the good and the best: a distinction not always clearly defined, thus making the choice difficult.

The second hindrance—sin—while more easily definable, is hard to throw off. It 'clings so closely'. We need to take radical steps to turn away from our sin and to turn to God in repentance and faith. Difficult though the race may be, Jesus has run it before us. He will be with us to strengthen us.

Lord, help us to throw off every weight and the sin that clings so closely. May we run the race with perseverance.

BA

Joy!

Let us run with perseverance the race that is set before us, looking to Jesus... who for... the joy that was set before him endured the cross, disregarding its shame.

Any mother knows from personal experience that, once she has her baby in her arms, the pain of giving birth fades into oblivion, to be replaced by joy. During his life on earth, Jesus focused on the joy that was awaiting him in his Father's presence. This anticipated joy enabled him to endure suffering and that ignominious death on the cross. He looked beyond the suffering, beyond the cross, beyond death. This does not mean that his suffering was in any way diminished. If he was able to 'disregard' the shame of the cross, it is only as he compares it to 'the joy that was set before him', which far outweighs the shame.

The fact that we are to run the race 'with perseverance' should warn us that it will not be easy. At times we may feel like giving up, but we are encouraged to persevere, to endure. We too can look beyond the trials of this world to that 'eternal weight of glory beyond all measure' which our 'slight momentary affliction is preparing us for' (2 Corinthians 4:17). Our 'affliction', which may in fact be severe and ongoing, is only qualified as 'slight and momentary' in comparison to the 'eternal weight of glory beyond all measure'. The apostle Paul is in no way minimizing what we have to endure in this life. But he turns our gaze heavenward and enables us to focus on eternal, spiritual realities.

Do we have this perspective? Are we looking beyond our suffering to the one in whose presence 'there is fullness of joy' (Psalm 16:11)?

Lord, we confess that we find it hard to rejoice in our trials. We thank you for Jesus who looked beyond the cross to the joy he would experience in your presence. Help us not to focus on our problems, but to lift our eyes and look to you.

BA

Training

The Lord disciplines those whom he loves.

Discipline. Not a very popular concept! Painful, undesirable, constricting, discipline goes against the grain and our natural inclination to laziness. The very word conjures up half-forgotten memories of strict teachers at school dispensing sanctions, or of severe parents punishing for wrong-doing. Discipline is definitely something we could do without!

Is it really? This passage seems to indicate otherwise. True, it does say that 'discipline always seems painful rather than pleasant *at the time*'. But if the discipline itself is painful, let us then focus rather on its *results*, and see if it is not worth it in the long run.

We have all been around indisciplined children—and maybe suffered the consequences of their bad behaviour! Lack of discipline leads to lack of respect. Parents who lovingly and fairly discipline their children will earn their respect (v. 9).

In this passage, it is 'the discipline of the Lord' that the writer is referring to. And that makes all the difference, for even though our human parents 'disciplined us as seemed best to them', they were not perfect. But we know that the Lord is perfectly just and loving. In fact, the Lord disciplines us *because* he loves us; his discipline is proof that we are his children (vv. 7 and 8). And his discipline is never arbitrary, but always purposeful and constructive: it is 'for our good, in order that we may share his holiness' (v. 10). Even though it is painful while we are going through it, 'later it yields the peaceful fruit of righteousness to those who have been trained by it'.

So, discipline is part of God's training programme to make us holy and righteous—in other words, to make us like Jesus.

Thank you, Lord, that I am your child and that you love me enough to discipline me. I thank you that through it you are training me, so that I will become more like Jesus. Help me to see my trials in this perspective.

BA

Strengthened through storms

Lift your drooping hands and strengthen your weak knees.

Here we have a picture of despondency and discouragement. It reminds me of the robin in that childhood rhyme:

The north wind doth blow
And we shall have snow.
And what will poor robin do then, poor thing?
He'll sit in a barn
And keep himself warm
And hide his head under his wing, poor thing.

Wind, snow, rain or hail, robins round our way—together with sparrows, tits, chaffinches, blackbirds, and even a pair of turtle doves—seem ready enough to hold their heads high and brave the elements. No hiding in barns for them! Maybe their intrepid confrontation with nature has something to do with the nuts and seeds hanging from our cherry tree. Be that as it may, there they are, not running away from, but courageously facing the winds and storms.

I wonder how we measure up to those little birds? At the first sign of hardship and buffetting, do we run away and hide, with our heads under our metaphorical wings, or do we face the storms of life with head held high? Maybe the storm is within, caused by our sinful nature 'with its passions and desires' (Galatians 5:24), making us hang our heads in shame. Perhaps it is without, and takes the form of trials and sorrows that come upon us unbidden, causing us to suffer in solitude and silence. No matter what the origin of the storm may be, if we are in Christ we can know his peace; we can stand tall and face it head on, assured of forgiveness and cleansing and victory over sin; confident of his presence with us; knowing that his 'strength is made perfect in weakness' (2 Corinthians 12:9, AV).

Thank you, Lord, for your victory over sin; thank you for your promise of forgiveness and cleansing. Thank you that your strength is made perfect in my weakness. Help me to live in the light of your promises.
BA

Pursue peace and holiness

Pursue peace with everyone, and the holiness without which no one will see the Lord.

'Peace on earth' seems rather an elusive commodity, to say the least! We only have to look at the news to see fighting in many parts of the world. Envy, greed, hatred, desire for revenge, on a national level and between individuals, make for a world where peace is at best precarious.

But surely things are different in our churches? Here at least there can be no such problems! Alas—how sad it is that we hear of splits and divisions within the Church. Let us determine, in so far as it depends on us, to 'live peaceably with all' (Romans 12:18).

The verbs used by the writer of the letter to the Hebrews would indicate that things are not simple and straightforward. *Pursue* peace, *strive* for it, *make every effort* to live harmoniously with others. Even within the context of the local church, peace cannot be taken for granted: it has to be worked at. We need to be intently single-minded in our pursuit.

We are also exhorted to strive after holiness in the same way. The Bible has a strong emphasis on holy living. 'As he who called you is holy, be holy yourselves in all your conduct for it is written, "You shall be holy, for I am holy"' (1 Peter 1:15, 16). To be holy means to be 'set apart' for God, and therefore presupposes separation from sin and anything that would be displeasing to God. As God's own people, we are a 'holy nation' (1 Peter 2:9).

Lord, when we look around us, we are saddened by the strife and dissension in the world. We regret the lack of peace among your children. Forgive me for my critical and judgmental attitude; for my argumentative and competitive spirit. May I truly 'seek peace and pursue it'. Lord, you have called us to be holy. Help me to turn my back on sin and to live for you.

'If we confess our sins, he who is faithful and just will forgive us our sins and cleanse us from all unrighteousness' (1 John 1:9).

BA

Keep on loving

Let mutual love continue.

I still remember, as a child at school, excitedly embarking upon a new activity: weaving. I confess to my shame that the initial enthusiasm soon wore off and I never did finish the piece of work I had so readily begun. It is sometimes difficult, after having begun the Christian life with great enthusiasm, to maintain the momentum. Many times in scripture we are urged to continue, to keep going, to persevere in one or other aspect of Christian living.

I believe we will only be able to keep on in this way in so far as we are being renewed in our faith daily. We need to feed on God's word each day. Last year or last month; last week—or even yesterday—is not enough. Today is what counts. And the nourishment we receive today is for today. Tomorrow we must feed again. For the children of Israel in the desert, the manna could not be stored up. God provided for them afresh each day. And so he does for us. 'His mercies... are new every morning' (Lamentations 3:23). Jesus taught us to pray, 'Give us this day our daily bread' (Matthew 6:11).

The Bible has a lot to say about loving one another. 'This is the message you have heard from the beginning,' says the apostle John, 'that we should love one another' (1 John 3:11). And this is, in fact, the commandment given by Jesus himself to his disciples: 'Just as I have loved you, you also should love one another' (John 13:34).

The writer of this letter to the Hebrews had already assured his readers (in 6:10) that God would not overlook 'the love that you showed for his sake in serving the saints as you still do'. And here, at the end of his letter, he encourages them to keep on loving. Love is costly: it takes time, energy. It cost Jesus his life. It can be emotionally draining. We may be tempted many times to give up.

Let us examine our hearts before the Lord: do we love one another as he loved us, with a self-giving love that never gives up?

BA

Contentment

Be content with what you have.

Taken out of context, these words could seem a command to instant contentment. This may not surprise us, though, as we are so used to having everything 'instant'—from coffee to practically every kind of 'mix'!

But God does not usually work that way. Take the unfolding of the seasons, for example. It takes a long time for the sleep of winter to give way to the new life of spring, and even longer for fruit to ripen and come to maturity. God works in the same way in the lives of his children. It would seem that his transforming work is always progressive—a process, often long.

The apostle Paul writes: 'I have *learned* to be content with whatever I have... In any and all circumstances I have *learned* the secret of being well fed and of going hungry, of having plenty and of being in need' (Philippians 4:11, 12). This was no instant contentment, but the result of a learning process.

Along the same lines, commenting on Psalm 131, Sinclair Ferguson (in *Deserted by God?*, Banner of Truth) describes the struggles and trauma of the weaning process evoked for us by the psalmist in verse 2: ' I have stilled and quieted my soul; like a weaned child with its mother, like a weaned child is my soul within me.' He says we will find true contentment by submitting to God's will. As weaned infants we have to lose the milk we desire to receive solid food. 'So too in the world of the Spirit: the weaning that brings us to contentment in the Lord takes place through loss. Every experience in life in which we are deprived of what we naturally want becomes the means by which our Father gives us what he knows we really need.'

Let us examine our hearts before God: are we hankering after what we do not have, or are we learning to be content with what we do have?

BA

Proverbs 1:2 (GNB)

Solomon's cook book

Here are proverbs that will help you to recognize wisdom and good advice, and understand sayings with deep meaning.

How wonderful it is to delve into one of those glorious illustrated cookery books where the sprouts glisten and the fruit pies seep glossy juices that positively make your mouth water. The down side is that the next time I produce dull vegetables and burnt crumble I feel even more of a failure as a cook than I did before. The up side is that I have a picture of what I am striving for and a knowledge that someone somewhere knows how to do it!

Now I haven't looked at Proverbs before—not properly. I haven't sat down with my mug of coffee and enjoyed it. Today I did and found my spirit hungry for the kind of wisdom described here so attractively. Not dry and overcooked, or limp and watery, but robust and tasty.

'If you listen to me you will know what is just and fair. You will know what you should do.' So much more challenging than some of the 'just ask and God will tell you' modern recipes for spiritual life.

Then there are the strenuous verses preaching against adultery and for marriage, and the verses telling us about the dangers of laziness and the value of friendship. Admittedly some of the sayings do seem rather simplistic and not always true to my experience. 'Storms come and the wicked are blown away but honest people are always safe' just doesn't wash unless you think in terms of life being eternal, as Solomon probably does.

Overall I was overwhelmed by the feeling that all the advice was being offered by someone who believed in a loving God who, in the words of 3:12, is 'proud' of his 'child'.

Over the next fortnight we are going to delve into some of the advice but before we do I suggest a mug of coffee, a comfy chair and a good old read.

Dear Father, write the recipes you want us to try on our hearts.

                                                                    BP

Kill or cure

Singing to a person who is depressed is like taking off his clothes on a cold day or like rubbing salt in a wound.

So that's where the phrase 'rub salt into the wound' comes from. In this context some of the usual sermons extolling the virtues of salt (it hurts to heal, and so on) seem inappropriate.

It is clearly not just silly but positively cruel to jolly along someone who is profoundly unhappy. They are already shivering outside the door. They are already in pain.

We are the Lord's hands. How can we help those who are struggling through a blizzard? Certainly not by cheerfully setting out to convince our travellers that they are happy and warm. In fact they often don't need words at all. They need a refuge.

For our young daughter this takes the form of a hot bubbly bath, a cuddle in front of a comfortable television programme or a silly old board game. She needs reassurance that she will be all right again but also acceptance that right now she isn't, and respect for the courage she will have to find to face life again

For a young friend recently home from the psychiatric ward of our local hospital, it's chocolate, gentlest teasing and trips to teddy bear shops. She needs reassurance that she will be better one day, but that right now we take seriously that every day requires courage and that her immediate future does not look very orange.

An elderly relative, facing the rapid winding down of his active life, needs the same reassurance. In the words of Julian of Norwich, 'All will be well and all manner of things will be well.' But right now it doesn't feel like that. He wants to know, through the way we treat him, that the crises he faces have weight in our eyes.

Dear Father, help us to find a way to provide warmth and shelter from the storm for those whom you buffet in our direction.

BP

A sticky story

Depending on an unreliable person in a crisis is like trying to chew with a loose tooth.

The dreaded toffee tale! Characters: a tooth and a toffee. Moral: misery is created by conveniently setting aside the truth. Plot: we have a weak tooth. We should have gone to the dentist months ago. Eating is a misery. A friend has a bag of toffees. We *so* like toffees…! Even though we know that toffees like to take trophies in their war against tooth survival and that our dependence on them will mean an expensive trip to the dentist, we set common sense aside and succumb to temptation. Within seconds we realize what has happened, but it is too late. We, or rather our tooth, is stuck with the choice we have made!

It can be like that in a crisis. The problem can be that we do not want to go to someone sensible, because we are afraid that they will judge us for our role in creating the problem. If only we had listened to them earlier, the crisis could have been minimized. Now we cannot face the inevitable reprimand so we turn to someone at least as weak as us. Someone who will fudgily tell us it isn't our fault, who will offer us tacky advice that will make the situation many times stickier. And when everything has turned out disastrously we know in our hearts we will have to seek the help of our wiser adviser anyway. We are so daft, aren't we?

Moral: the experience of most of us is that even if he hurts you a bit, a good dentist can help you get your smile back.

Dear Father, there are times when we don't want to come to you because we know what you will say. Help us today to look seriously at those on whom we rely. Are they the people that in our hearts we think you would have chosen for us at this time? If not, give us the courage to resist their advice and to turn to you.

BP

Forest fires

Without wood, a fire goes out; without gossip, quarrelling stops. Charcoal keeps the embers glowing, wood keeps the fire burning, and troublemakers keep arguments alive.

This image expresses the very opposite to the favourite kindling used by gossips, the notorious 'There's no smoke without fire'.

So what actually happens ? How is the fire lit? When I was a Girl Guide a million years ago, one of our badges involved cooking outside over an open fire. First we collected 'punk' (discarded silver birch bark) and made a tiny pile, over which we carefully placed our twigs. I can't remember ever successfully keeping one of my little fires going for more than a few minutes, except on one occasion when my fellow chef surreptitiously slid a bought firelighter into the centre of the little pile of smouldering bark. The effect was instantaneous and, despite my guilt, our sausages burnt victoriously. Quarrels can flare up so easily, but often they would die down as quickly as my pathetic little attempts if it wasn't for the addition of slow-burning gossip fuel.

We are worried. We care about our friends. We decide to share our anxiety. After all, where's the harm in that? How extraordinary, they have been wondering too... Together you marvel at your two minds thinking alike and warm your hands over the small fire, blowing on the truth slightly to fan the flames, throwing a few more twigs in for good measure. Something you've heard they said, or didn't say, did or didn't do. Seeing the fire begin to die down, you call someone else to throw on fuel. It's so cosy being part of the group warming their hands. It's not our responsibility. They're the ones who caused it.

But unless we actively stamp out the embers, our fire will spread like... well yes, like wildfire, devouring everything in its path. Too late we will be forced to witness the devastating scars our harmless little blaze has caused.

Dear Father, help us to bring water, not fuel, to the fires of quarrels.
BP

Naughty but nice

Gossip is so tasty! How we love to swallow it!

I hate gossip! I also gossip! It is, as this proverb observes with frightening accuracy, so *tasty*. The New International Version talks of 'choice morsels' which 'go down to a man's inmost parts'. Naughty but nice.

And indeed, what goodies are to be found in gossip. There's a certain piquancy about the risk, and a saltiness to being the one in the know. It feels delightfully indulgent, like succumbing with a friend to eating cakes oozing with cream. There is something intoxicating, like wine, about the power it brings. And perhaps more than all of these individual treats, there is the sense of close fellowship usually reserved to those occasions when we share a meal or meet for a drink with friends. But if you are anything like me, the whole thing, while tasting wonderful at the time, is very indigestible and leaves a disgusting taste in your mouth afterwards.

Why? The answer is quite simple really. Basically because it is not made of wholesome ingredients. It is forbidden fruit because it is bad for us and the apparent closeness is a substitute for real friendship, based on the same unity found in a group of addicts sharing a needle filled with a substance which, while giving them an instant high, will poison them all eventually.

Jesus said, 'My food is to do the will of my Father,' and he spent his life bringing about healing. Gossip will not help us to grow strong; it will poison our relationships. As it says elsewhere in Proverbs, 'Gossip separates close friends' and 'Gossip brings anger just as surely as the north wind brings rain.' Incidentally, it also says, 'Pleasant words are like a honeycomb, sweet to the soul and healing to the bones.'

Decide once and for all to go on a gossip-free diet, not just for today but for ever.

Dear Father, help us to be strong, and give us courage to resist the temptation to feast at the devil's table.

                                                                    BP

On the roof

A nagging wife is like water going drip-drip-drip on a rainy day. How can you keep her quiet? Have you ever tried to stop the wind or ever tried to hold a handful of oil? ... Better to live on the roof than share the house with a nagging wife.

Somehow you just know this is written by a man! 'Naggravation' seems to be the current term for what is still considered all these years later to be the bane of these poor hard-done-by husbands! Rather live on the roof, eh? Well, that's fine so long as the roof's not falling to bits because the poor downtrodden mate hasn't got round to repairing it! Nagging is still up there with mother-in-law jokes yet, amazingly, still seems to be politically correct. The question is: who finds it funny when they really think about it? Not the husband. Not the wife. Certainly not the children.

I recently heard it described as an unacceptable exertion of power. What do you think of that? In my experience it's more likely to be women expressing hurt that what is important to them (like mending the tap that goes drip-drip-drip!) is not given the same priority as demands from outside the home— from work, from church, from mates.

Nagging is probably one of the most destructive weapons the devil uses in his fight against marriage. And like anything originating from his infernal joke factory, the joke is on us. As long as he has a husband and wife involved in sparring matches and retiring after each bout increasingly bloodied, feeling misunderstood and undervalued, he will be the only one laughing. Incidentally, if this is happening not to you but to someone you care about, don't just be there in their corner dabbing their wounds, wiping their foreheads and whispering encouragement ready for the next bout. Remember the devil will be the only overall champion.

Dear Father, show us how to bind up the wounds and start again.

BP

Bird catchers

Curses cannot hurt you unless you deserve them. They are like birds that fly by and never settle.

Have you noticed that for some reason we just don't seem able to let them fly by? There we are out with our long-handled catching-nets, determined that each one is for us. We cradle it in our hands, keeping it alive and jealously claiming it for our own. Why? Why do we feed on criticism and bad feeling? To damn ourselves? On one memorable evening our housegroup all shared their inner conviction that they seriously believed they were not only the tares among the wheat but also probably wolves in sheep's clothing, bad yeast and unfruitful fig trees. In fact, just about everything that their Saviour abhorred.

Another proverb chillingly states that a good person who gives in to someone who is evil reminds you of a polluted spring or a poisoned well. Is this not what we are doing when we claim curses for our own? When we refuse to accept that forgiveness means that we are purified of all? It is like deliberately putting a drop of poison into the sparkling water of love and forgiveness that Jesus constantly pours into us. Well, it's about time we became a little more environmentally friendly towards ourselves and stopped being so silly. Let's take this business about curses flying past seriously, wave them goodbye, pull down our catching-nets and use them to clean out the scum collecting on the surface of our well.

Dear Lord, with your help we can do it.

                                                           BP

Capable or what!

How hard it is to find a capable wife! She is worth far more than jewels!

Well, if this paragon of all virtue, common sense and skill is what the writer sees as 'capable', no wonder it is so hard to find one!

What a lady! If she's not spinning and weaving, she's scouring the land for tasty titbits for her husband or planting vines or selling belts or looking after the kids. Wow! But wait. Haven't I met her? Isn't she simply trying to be what many, many women are expected to be today? Running a home and family, pursuing a career, cooking superb foreign meals, trying to still be there for her friends. But there are differences. One is that there is the mention of servants. Presumably this ideal lady isn't actually doing the rough. Maybe that's why she seems so calm. Or maybe it's something else. She is *praised* for what she does. For many nowadays it is the norm. No praise. And, for many women, no husband to give the praise. A single friend of mine was describing her daily dash between her job, her daughter's school, son's child-minder, shops and home as a nightmare from which she never wakes up. 'I'm always running, always arriving a few minutes late to absolutely everything, trying to look as though I've actually been there on time, feeling guilty.' When I told her how well I thought she was doing, she burst into tears.

I'm not and never have been the ideal wife, mother or, indeed, daughter. I'm not proud of it. All my life I've yearned and tried to be more organized, less frantic and more capable. But I'm not. I'm just me. I know I've said it before, but the incredible thing for me and for you is that that is enough for God to see us as more precious than jewels.

Dear Father, we so want to be good at what we do. Today as we chunter along at full speed, help us to feel we sparkle in your eyes.

BP

Juggling priorities

Do what is right and fair; that pleases the Lord more than bringing him sacrifices.

It sounds so simple, doesn't it? Yet it is one of the things that probably causes women most anxiety. How do you treat each child exactly the same? How do you balance the time you spend with your husband, children, parents and friends? Is it right and fair to take on work for the church or the community if you are already busy? If you don't, someone else will have to. It is the juggling of priorities that is so exhausting.

When Adrian's mum first suffered a stroke and was in hospital twenty miles away, I visited daily for months. Every day was an obstacle race, trying to make my mother-in-law feel as though I had all the time in the world while watching the clock ready to leap into the car, charge into the shops, fume behind the inevitable tractor, and arrive outside the school gates invariably a few minutes late before getting home to all the work four children create. At that stage I wasn't also having to fit in a full-time job, being an unpaid secretary for my husband, but even so during that time I think I experienced 'life rage'! It was a constant feeling that every day I was setting out to build a domino chain and that at some point, however carefully I constructed it, something would happen to make the whole jolly lot fall over. At times like this, we need to note that God values our effort to be just and fair more than sacrifices.

Tonight, before you go to bed, write down all the events of the day, including all your mental tussles, and offer them to him. He says it will give him pleasure. If you are too worn out from trying to be just and fair to have the time or energy for this, just go to sleep trusting that God is smiling at your domino pile.

                                                                    BP

God's maps

The Lord has determined our path; how then can anyone understand the direction his own life is taking?

'It's not my fault. It's this stupid map. They've put in a whole new one-way street system since this was made. It's impossible to go down that road.'

I was miserably sharing the back seat with several large boxes of books, listening to my husband and a friend who was driving us to a speaking engagement getting more and more worked up as we repeatedly shot past the turning where we could see, tantalizingly, the hall at which we should already be joining in the fun. I groaned, picturing one hundred and fifty harvest suppers waiting limply under their clingfilm for our arrival. But Adrian was right. The map they'd sent was out of date.

We get lost all the time but I don't think that God has sent us the wrong map, or that he doesn't actually care that we struggle so much to find our way.

I do think that God continually changes the road layouts of our lives. Unless we are constantly checking with him where we should be going, we are bound to get lost, but I think he reroutes us with purpose.

I think our world must be rather like the sort of map you see in police dramas where coloured drawing-pins denote the spots where tragedies have taken place. But God's map is intending that intervention will actually prevent many of the tragedies taking place. He only has a limited number of folk listening to him so he has to use his resources as best he can. He needs someone to be somewhere for someone all the time. Of course we don't know where our path is leading, because we don't know where there is a need and where he will need us to be.

Next time we find ourself in what seems to be a dead-end street, maybe we ought to look around before we put all our efforts into getting out as soon as possible.

BP

Polishing the harness

You can get horses ready for battle, but it is the Lord who gives victory.

The other Sunday I was on the rota to do the prayers at church. Over the last two years I have felt increasingly free to pray spontaneously for the needs of our church family. At first, standing up in front of the congregation without notes was a genuine stepping-out in faith and an awareness of the immense privilege I had been given. I would diligently read the newspapers to discover the world's needs, check with our minister what we, as a congregation, needed to petition our Father for and search my heart prayerfully. Throughout the service I would be trying to hear what God might be prompting me to say and when I stood up I would be shaking with nerves at the responsibility of my task and beg my heavenly Father to give me the words. Over the months it got easier, I got lazier and this time I caught myself out. At the moment when I realized what my job was to be on this particular Sunday, I actually heard my inner voice saying, 'Oh great, nothing to prepare!'

Of course, it is the Lord who gives any victory we appear to achieve in our spiritual battles. But if the horses were underfed and exhausted they would be less able to aid their human's cause and bring about the right victory. Lazy polishing of harnesses might not appear to have the same level of importance but shining tack would glint in the sun and reflect the pride and confidence in the justice of their cause. God has harnessed his absolute power to our feeble spiritual frames. The least we can do is to make sure they are prepared for his use.

Dear Father, show us what we need to muck out, and how we can increase the health of our spiritual lives so that we no longer look like tubby Thelwell ponies and we can be used by you to help bring about your victory.

BP

Knowing me, knowing you

*I ask you, God, to let me have two things before I die: keep me
from lying, and let me be neither rich nor poor. So give me
only as much food as I need. If I have more, I might say that I
do not need you. But if I am poor, I might steal and bring disgrace on my God.*

What I like so much in this proverb are the words 'I might'.
There is no claimed victory but an acknowledgment of vulnerability at the root of human nature and acceptance that we must
live realistically with our particular weaknesses in order to overcome them.

A friend of ours has two sons who both want to give up smok-
ing. To one he offered a huge incentive at the end of a year of
non-smoking. He knew this son would be unable to bear the
guilt of cheating on his father. He was right. The written promise
was kept by his bed to strengthen his resolve nightly. His second
son was inspired to take up the same challenge. Being more
impusive and generous, he also had much weaker resolve. He
was crestfallen to hear that his father had no intention of repeating the challenge, until it was explained.

'Because you are very like me I know it could be too much of
a burden and might cause you to lie to me. I reckon the poison
of those lies would be worse for you than the nicotine.' Shorter
term goals and regular successes were needed for him.

I'm the same with dieting. It's no good me buying a size 10
dress as a long-term incentive; I end up hating it and getting fat-
ter! To keep me going I need little treats if I am good for a week!
Pathetic? Yes, maybe, but true for me and the truth has always
set us free as Jesus said it would.

*Father, help me to trust you know exactly the amount of daily bread I
need to keep me from greed or complacency.*

BP

Safe and sound

It is dangerous to be concerned with what others think of you but if you trust the Lord, you are safe.

Safe. That is such a lovely word, isn't it?

For years, one of our sons struggled at school with the feeling that whatever he did he was thought silly. Having a Christian speaker for a dad hardly helped at the sort of school he was in. At the end of the day he would fling himself home, divest himself as soon as possible of bags and uniform and everything else associated with school and settle down on to the oldest, comfiest sofa in front of the television to be safe. He learnt later that his schoolmates thought none of the negative things he had attributed to them and indeed were fond of him, but he was such fun to tease because he always reacted. They have also told him how fed up they used to feel that he refused to join the rugby and football teams which would have benefited from his talent.

A little while ago I met the father of a friend of mine. He, by contrast, cared nothing for what other people felt about him. He strode through life delivering what he saw as truth and discipline. If people reacted negatively, it was probably because they were at fault. His determination to be unaffected by the opinion of others meant that he hurt and wounded folk wherever he went, especially his family.

Clearly, neither of these extremes is desirable but it is human and right to be at least aware of the opinions of others. Without this awareness we can become indifferent to the needs of others and even cruel. The danger lies where it affects our ability to move forward; where we convince ourselves that no one wants or needs us; where we allow our world to be impoverished by our decision that we are not good enough.

Let us today feed on the comfort of knowing that we are safe in the Lord's appreciation of us.

BP

How to be a rain cloud

People who promise things that they never give are like clouds and wind that bring no rain.

Memories of childhood outings seemed always to include my mother's decidedly optimistic declaration that there 'was just enough blue sky to make a Dutch man a pair of trousers' as we set out for summer picnics armed with umbrellas and warmest woollies! I grew up with the distinct impression that all Dutch men must be tiny!

Years later, when touring Australia, I was able to appreciate the significance of this sort of illusion. We were sitting on the veranda of a beautiful house in Goondawindi besieged by the relentless afternoon heat, when there was a small gasp from our hostess. We followed her hand as she pointed out a tiny, wispy, grey cloud.

'I'm sorry,' she said sadly, as we resumed our tea. 'It's just that we haven't had any rain for so many months. Grey clouds promise rain and we find ourselves praying every time that just this once it will fulfil its promise over our town. It never does.' We had seen the effects of the drought all too clearly. Dead crops. Scrawny cattle just about surviving on the verges of the dusty roads. Farmers at the end of their resources, buying water at enormous cost. For them it would have felt literally as if the heavens opened if they had had some rain.

We make wispy promises constantly and we so often don't keep them. Why? God kept his ultimate promise of reconciliation by sending his Son because he 'so loved the world'. Is this the clue? Is it to do with the weight of our love? Is our concern so burdensome that only the fulfilling of our promise would lighten our load?

Dear Father, bound up in the amazing mystery of your love is that our trust, our prayers and our love for our fellow men and women enable you to bring them relief. Forgive us for the many times we have prevented your blessed rain.

BP

Luke 1:32–33 (NRSV)

History makers

*He will be great, and will be called the Son of the Most High,
and the Lord God will give to him the throne of his ancestor
David. He will reign over the house of Jacob forever, and of
his kingdom there will be no end*

The new millennium dawns—calendars across most of the world
recognize it. A global fuss is about to overtake us, ranging from
doomsday prophecies to wild parties, from souvenir domes to
computer bugs which threaten to bring to a standstill the tech-
nology we rely on every day. But who knows why? If this is about
the numbers 999 changing to 000, surely we have lost the plot!

Few except Christians recognize that we're celebrating the
pivotal time of history—two thousand years since the birth of a
baby changed BC to the 'Year of Our Lord'. So, if we're to com-
municate what we believe the millennium celebrations are all
about, we need to think hard. Most people acknowledge that,
though Jesus walked the earth for only thirty-three years, he
started *something*. But is world history really 'his story'? What difference have his followers made? Ah, that's the real challenge.
The first lot were an unpromising bunch, and now he's stuck
with the likes of you and me!

But isn't that the point? God has always worked with the
weakest. He singled out the shepherd boy David to fight a giant
and then to lead his nation. He spotlighted the passionately mis-
guided Paul. He risked sending his Son, not as an emperor, but
as a helpless baby. He chooses not zapping thunderbolts or
angels, but you and me to be part of 'his story'. Co-operating
with him, we can affect maybe not the history of the entire planet, but the history of all those whose lives we touch.

*Think about all those weak or 'ordinary' characters in the Bible, his-
tory and contemporary life whom God has used to make a difference
in this world. Then ask him to remind you of times when he has used
you too!*

CL

God changing my own history

And he said: 'I tell you the truth, unless you change and become like little children, you will never enter the kingdom of heaven.'

I often wonder why God chose me to follow Jesus. I know many people far more lovable (and loving) who aren't even Christians.

If God asks me to follow Jesus in making a little bit of history, even if that's 'merely' telling someone else about him, I tend to run away. That's because I have mountains of faith in my own ability to mess things up, and I can think of a million people who would do better than me. I'd make any situation worse—put enquirers off for ever, bring the noblest of projects into disrepute.

The disciples had been squabbling about who would be greatest in God's kingdom. Generalizations aren't helpful, but isn't it interesting that they were men? I'm not guilty of their particular sin, nor are most women I know, and yet we also need to change and become like trusting children. The disciples had not yet grasped that *anyone* submitting to God's fatherly rule becomes his beloved child—amazingly valued, amazingly important to him. I'm just as bad, when effectively I say to God, 'You've made a mistake. I'm not like your other children. I'm useless. I can see them learning to ride bikes, swim, do the dishes, help the homeless and preach the gospel in foreign lands. But, even with your help, I'm sure to mess up all your plans.'

My thinking needs radical change if it's to line up with God's. I mean, what was the most momentous moment in history—and whom did Jesus choose to reveal it to the world? A woman, a prostitute, who had little understanding, yet knew that she was loved and forgiven—and who was there!

Dear Jesus, show me what stops me becoming a good protagonist in your story. I come before you like a child, in trust and humility. Set me free to do your will! Amen

CL

Esther 4:14 (NRSV)

For such a time as this!

For if you keep silence at such a time as this, relief and deliverance will rise for the Jews from another quarter, but you and your father's family will perish. Who knows? Perhaps you have come to royal dignity for just such a time as this.

The Jews had been carted off as captives of a king whose rule was absolute over lands which stretched from India to Ethiopia. When his wife misbehaved, he banished her and demanded beautiful virgins, one per night. Lined up to await her turn, Jewish orphan Esther could have disappeared for ever, the victim of circumstances, like so many before her. Yet out of the whole harem, she won the king's favour and was made queen.

I wonder how she felt? Betrayed? Jews weren't supposed to get involved in mixed marriages. Isolated and lonely away from her own people? This was no marriage of companionable support. Afraid? The king had absolute power, and courtiers envied her prosperity.

Then, through machinations and deceit within the court, her own people came under the death sentence—all of them. Would Esther accept defeat resignedly, letting circumstances win, letting the helplessness of her past become her future? Or would she see the hand of God at work and choose to trust him more than she trusted her own fear of the king? What would you have done?

Esther didn't rush into hasty action but nor was she paralysed by indecision. She knew there was no guarantee of winning through; she knew that she might perish. The future of her people rested on her shoulders. She believed that if she failed them now, God would send another rescuer, but even so, she didn't side-step. Maybe he *had* brought her to royal dignity for such a time as this!

Lord, for all your people who feel that circumstances conspire against them, grant a vision of yourself as history maker. Give hope that you will use their suffering to enable them to rescue others. Amen

CL

Preparations

On the third day Esther put on her royal robes and stood in the inner court of the king's palace, opposite the king's hall.

Invited onto the committee of the Association of Christian Writers, I spun into my 'they've got the wrong person' routine. Surely they'd mistaken me for another Christine Leonard! But God didn't let me get away with that and soon I found myself not only contributing new ideas, but having to give talks in front of halls full of people.

Beforehand I sweated and felt sure I'd be sick. As I attempted to speak into the microphone, my voice wouldn't work properly—that's if my legs allowed me to reach the front in the first place. Though I didn't carry the lives of a nation on my shoulders like Esther, ACW's vision was not small. At the bare minimum, if we could train and inspire one person to write one sentence in a local magazine, and if God breathed into it to change the life of one person, that person, with God, *could* go on to change the nation.

Esther fasted for three days and asked the Jews to fast too. Then she made thoughtful preparations, dressing herself in royal robes, cooking sumptuous banquets for the King and Haman. I booked myself on an adult education course in public speaking. And I prayed—it's not hard to pray when you fall in at the deep end! The dreaded course did help, becoming a necessary preparation for what God was asking of me. Other preparations he made himself without my realizing it, notably putting others alongside me to help and teach and pray. For Esther he arranged things so that the king read a book which reminded him how her uncle had foiled an attempt on his own life—and had never been rewarded.

In his own good time, the Lord of history does answer the prayers of those who find themselves out of their depth in 'his story'.

Read the book of Esther.

CL

We are the dreamers of dreams

Where there is no vision, the people perish.

The church leader had reached a point of exasperation with us that night. 'We serve this church,' he said, 'we love one another and our families, we teach our children about Jesus—and a handful of our neighbours too. We try to be kind to everyone and stay away from sin. We love God, study the Bible, pray hard and give generously. But is that what it's all about?'

Well, yes, I thought, alarmed that he implied something different. He didn't explain further and the question continued to bother me. Had I missed the point of my faith? What did Jesus do? He explained his mission as bringing good news to the poor, releasing captives, making the blind see and freeing the oppressed. I knew he still cared passionately about doing those things through his people in my church, my family, my street, but maybe my view was limited. If Christians stayed in cosy corners —if they never asked God what part they might play in his wider vision for the world, if they never dared ask him for dreams and stepped out of their comfort zones in faith to make them happen—his kingdom would be mighty slow in coming!

All the things in the first paragraph are foundational to Christians and foundations are vital, but only if they support a useful building. Jesus gave us just two commandments. If we love God fully we'll make ourselves available to be part of *his* vision— then we may find ourselves loving some surprising neighbours. They may not be on our heart right now, but they are on his!

God's heart and vision are astronomically bigger than anything I can comprehend. Perhaps I can ask him to expand me, little by little, until I begin to recognize, then get involved in, that particular bit of his wider story-line where someone like me really could make a difference.

Your kingdom come, Lord, your will be done on earth as it is in heaven.

CL

History-making heroes

Therefore, since we are surrounded by so great a cloud of witnesses, let us also lay aside every weight and the sin that clings so closely, and let us run with perseverance the race that is set before us.

Read Hebrews 11 and let the history-making heroes of faith in the Old Testament inspire you. Spend time looking into the face of Jesus, the 'pioneer and perfecter of our faith'. Then run with him.

Simple, isn't it? But I find it hard to identify with blood sacrifices and ark-building, and our culture honours few more recent history-making 'witnesses'. My children's living heroes came from pop or sport or film—famous but ephemeral—and out of their reach. Kids might dream of breaking an Olympic record or of attaining Superman's mega-stardom, but, realistically, it won't happen. God's heroes, on the other hand, are ordinary, often inadequate people. By faith, some change history.

I started collecting stories of living heroes—and filled several books with them. An Ulsterman who established the fastest growing church in West Africa insisted his achievements weren't worth the telling because he lacked education. A home-loving nurse from Cheshire found herself a lone, short-term foreign volunteer in a Romanian hospital full of abandoned children dying of AIDS. She prayed, she modelled Jesus' love—and saw not only that but other hospitals transformed. She kept protesting, 'If you knew me, Chris, I'm such an ordinary person!' A tiny Sri Lankan, too shy to be accepted publicly into membership of her London church, shared the good news about Jesus with some of her own people—refugees in France and Switzerland. Ex-Tamil Tigers, though transformed, weren't welcome in local churches, so she found herself with several churches of her own to look after. 'And women never lead anything in my culture, so it had to be God!' she said.

Father, we thank you for all the heroes of faith who people your story as it unfolds, but especially for Jesus, the hero. Help us to follow him fully. Amen

CL

Which side's winning?

[Christ is] far above all rule and authority and power and dominion, and above every name that is named, not only in this age but also in the age to come. And he has put all things under his feet and has made him the head over all things for the church, which is his body, the fullness of him who fills all in all.

A university course in church history shook my faith more than any liberal theologian could. Only a few centuries after Jesus, Christians cut off the grain supply to a whole city because they disagreed with some point of theology being taught there. Crusaders slaughtered Moslems 'in the name of Jesus'—and no, we're not more civilized now, it happened in Bosnia. Adherents of different churches were killing and torturing each other in Northern Ireland, and what about the Inquisition? I began to wonder, was the Church part of God's story or Satan's?

Of course, individual Christians changed things for the better—Lord Shaftesbury, Elizabeth Fry, Wilberforce. Historians say the revivals led by the Wesleys and Whitfield prevented a bloodbath similar to the French Revolution. I began to see that there were groups, always, who kept the flame alight. Often they were the ones being persecuted, and if sometimes their stories lacked documentation, it was because they didn't always win. Not all in Hebrews 11 'won' either, in their lifetime. But God *will* win.

Historians may guess at what will happen in the future: they can't be certain. But more surely than we know that Poirot will get his man, or the Mills and Boon heroine hers, Christians know the end of 'his story'! It doesn't spoil the plot, because we don't know when or exactly *how* God will create a new heaven and a new earth. We do know they will contain no pain or crying or darkness or sin and that Christ will reign for ever, undisputed in glory.

When it comes to 'his story', I want to be on the winning side!

CL

God of hope

Therefore I am now going to allure her; I will lead her into the desert and speak tenderly to her. There I will give her back her vineyards, and will make the Valley of Achor a door of hope.

I couldn't understand how God could allow this door to be slammed in my face. I thought these people were my friends. We had worked together as colleagues for several years building 'the kingdom' together. Then a difference of opinion and a confrontation. And I was shut out. Ostracized. Cut off.

The pain was sharp and deep. These people and this Christian work had been my place to belong and to exercise the gifts God had given me. And now I was without a place to belong and without a place to minister. I felt like God had allured me into the desert solely to desert me. For what? Why?

In retrospect, many years later, I can see how God took what was so painful and difficult, a Valley of Achor (achor means 'trouble' or 'difficulty') and transformed it into a door of hope. And in retrospect, I can hear how tenderly he spoke to me in that valley of difficulty. For that 'shut door' caused me to return to university to study and to improve gifts God had given me which, in turn, has opened more doors for me to serve God.

Increasingly I discover that this is so like God. He doesn't just miraculously rescue us from our deserts, or whisk us immediately out of difficulty, but rather he transforms our troubles into hope. The valley becomes a door.

Dear God, help us to remember, when we are in our Valleys of Achor, that you will transform them into doors of hope.

EP

God of hope

There she will sing as in the days of her youth, as in the day she came up out of Egypt.

Do you remember your singing in the 'days of your youth'? Those days filled with carefree, curious discoveries as life unfolded before you?

I do. I remember long, intense, life-shaping conversations sitting on the grass at junior high school. I remember the laughter and the intimacy of friends. I remember the excitement, talking with other girls about what we were going to do. And what on earth we were going to do with our bodies, which were changing in scary and exciting ways. I remember the fun of those days… I also remember the trouble I got into when my exuberance got out of hand!

Even with the bits of life that weren't so good, they were still good days. We thought we could do anything. They were the days of the sixties when we, as young women, were being offered possibilities and opportunities undreamed of as yet. And yes, I was part of sit-ins and protests, naively thinking we could actually effect change.

In the past few years, I have had snatches of such experiences again. Warm, intimate, life-shaping conversations with women. Laughter and music—even in the deserts.

These verses talk about a renewal of that life-giving place of hope where we will sing as in the days of youth. A time when our Valleys of Achor will be changed into doors of hope where God will give us back the melodies of our youth.

God of hope, rejuvenate our brittle vocal chords to vibrate again with life and singing as we did as young girls and young women.

                                                                    EP

God of hope

*'In that day,' declares the Lord, 'you will call me "my
husband"; you will no longer call me "my master".'*

Last Sunday I was speaking to a group of 'pray-ers' at St James'
church in Toronto. We were reflecting on our personal understanding and experience of prayer.

I had been asked to describe my own prayer journey. I realized
that my image of God—and my experience of God—have
changed dramatically over the past forty years.

As a child and a teenager, my image of God was of a harsh,
demanding task-master, and a major party-poop. As an adult, I
now know God as energetically involved and interested in me
and my life. He is kind, loving, honest and gentle—and he loves
a good party. I know God as someone who cares deeply for me
and for all his people.

When I read these verses in Hosea, my experience affirms
that change in names. A change from role and function of master, to a role and function like that of husband. How very different these two roles and relationships are!

Master: a distant, hierarchical authority, not necessarily abu-
sive and oppressive but surely dominant and demanding.
Husband: an intimate, loving partner, affectionate and caring.
God as husband is bound by his commitment and covenant; he
knows and loves us in our nakedness; he walks by our side
through our Valleys of Achor, guiding us through those doors of
hope; he sings with us as in the days of our youth.

In these challenging days, we need a relationship of intimacy
and love and companionship with our God much more than we
need a master.

*God of intimate partnership, let us know how much you love us and
care for us today.*

                                                              EP

God of desires

For I desire mercy, not sacrifice, and acknowledgment of God rather than burnt offerings.

It's a bit strange thinking of God having desires, isn't it? Desires seem so fleshly, so human. When I read that God has desires, it stops me in my tracks. Human desires are often self-centred—what on earth would divine desires be centred on? God's desire in this verse has something to do with his relationship with us—he is actually desiring something from us!

I really do find it quite difficult at times to imagine that God wants anything from his relationship with us. I certainly know what I get out of it, but what does he get out of it? What can I *give* him that is of any worth? Mercy?

Now that's a challenge because we're often quite good, better in fact, at offering sacrifices—the *good deeds* of faith. But mercy, well, that's different! I remember one church we attended where the people were very well educated biblically with high commitment to the gospel, and clear obedience to the 'doing good' stuff. But they were also very judgmental and condemning, very insular from the world around them. These Christians had such a clear understanding of what they took to be the high calling of God, the standards of righteousness. But they were often unkind and uncaring, and at times downright nasty with one another and particularly with those who were not believers.

God desires mercy even more than sacrifice. That is very important to him. Kindness rather than harshness, love rather than condemnation, grace rather than nastiness.

Can we, this day, give God what he desires?

EP

God of desires

For I desire mercy, not sacrifice, and acknowledgment of God rather than burnt offerings.

My daughter has recently given birth to her first child. It has brought back all kinds of memories of the birth and raising of our own two daughters. The excitement of holding a newborn in my arms. The wonder of them drinking nourishment from my body. The fear of their soap-slippery little bodies escaping in the bath. Learning how they liked to be held and comforted. Knowing what pleased them and what agitated them. Watching them grow from babies to infants to children to young women. Continually discovering who they *are* as competent, beautiful women.

I have an understanding—a knowledge—of who they are. And the more I get to know them—'acknowledge' them—the more I like them and admire them. The more they get to know me, the more they understand me. This knowing and being known is one of the real delights of being human.

This parallels our experiences of getting to know God—or acknowledging God. These verses state that God *actually desires* that we have knowledge of him and that we *know* him in genuine relationship. This is more important to God than all the offerings we could give.

Not surprisingly, the more I get to know God, the more I like and adore him. The more I acknowledge him, the more I trust him with me. I don't exactly understand why God so desires that we *know* him, but what better desire to respond to in these crazy, millennium-end times than to know and acknowledge God for who he is!

Dear God, draw us into a deeper relationship with you.

EP

God of autumn rains

Blessed are those whose strength is in you, who have set their hearts on pilgrimage. As they pass through the Valley of Baca, they make it a place of springs; the autumn rains also cover it with pools. They go from strength to strength.

Valley of Baca—translated as valley of weeping; a valley lined with tombs.

Sometimes the evening news is just too difficult to watch. Sometimes listening to a friend's life experiences is just too painful. Our world seems at times to be littered with weeping and death. Death of hopes, of dreams, of plans; death of forgiveness, of reconciliation, of peace; death of innocent children, of loved ones, of good people.

Our personal pilgrimage through life inevitably leads us through 'Valleys of Baca'—valleys of weeping and of death. But there is hope, for I see God taking our wet, warm, abundant tears from weeping our pain and somehow transforming these tears into life-giving springs of water.

Have you ever noticed how strengthening our own 'death-experiences' can be to other pilgrims in the valley? Our own tears can create springs for them in their pain and weeping. Springs that nourish and strengthen. Springs that cleanse the salt-bitter taste of pain. Springs that soften hardened, parched soil bringing the possibility of new life.

These refreshing springs, that come from our own tears and weeping in the Valley of Baca, are further supplemented by the autumn rains. These are the rains that come from the heavens, showering and satisfying the parched, deadened ground. It is as if God's own tears for our loss and sorrow is added to ours, further watering the dryness of the pilgrims' valleys.

Dear God, source of life, keep us pilgrim-ing through the hard places. Take us from strength to strength.

EP

God of peace

*Peace I leave with you; my peace I give you. I do not give to
you as the world gives. Do not let your hearts be troubled and
do not be afraid.*

Jesus knew that his life on earth was quickly coming to an end.
He knew that the 'prince of this world' was coming for him (John
14:30). He knew that his disciples were anxious and afraid. Yet,
in the middle of his own need and his own fear, Jesus focused on
the needs of his disciples.

I can almost see the look in Jesus' eyes as he spoke to his disciples, as he told them of his own approaching death. Seeing
their agitation and their fear, feeling his own anxiety and fear.
And yet, in the middle of all this, looking with compassion and
tenderness on them. Once again, the mighty Prince of Peace
stepping outside his own need and serving them. And out of his
godly resource, at great personal cost, giving them his gift of
peace.

I wonder if he himself always lived with this peace? How did
he keep his heart from fear and being troubled? I don't know. But
I have had experiences of Jesus' gift of peace releasing my heart
from anxiety and fear. I don't live there all the time, but it is
remarkable when I do. And he is certainly calling us to live in
that peace. He urges us not to let our hearts be troubled and not
to be afraid because, at the same time, he promises that he will
not leave us as orphans—that he will come to us and dwell with
us (14:18).

*Oh dear Jesus, how we need you to come to us and give us peace.
Come today and meet our need.*

EP

God of peace

Peace I leave with you; my peace I give you. I do not give to you as the world gives.

If only I had a different supervisor, this office would be a lot more peaceful. If only the kids would stop arguing, our home would be a lot more peaceful. If only I had a different husband, I could really live in peace. If only I had a husband at all! And so it goes. Our litanies of 'if only's.

And true enough, if things or circumstances or people were different, then maybe our lives would be more peaceful. But these are the things and circumstances and people that make up our lives right now. Jesus calls us to 'grow where we are planted'. Thinking that peace is dependent on circumstances, dependent on those external things around us, is the nature of the peace the world offers us. It is not 'Jesus-peace'.

Jesus-peace is peace in the middle of the lives we have. In the middle of all the pressure and all the rubbish—it's here where this Jesus-peace works. It's not a peace from escaping or avoiding difficulties or from refusing to face reality. It is a peace that transforms us right in the middle of our very real lives!

This is the gift of peace from Jesus. In Hebrew, this peace is called *shalom*. *Shalom* never means simply the absence of trouble but it means the presence of God in the midst of the life-trash— all that is for our highest good. It is this gift of peace that enables us to work with a malicious supervisor. It is this gift that gives us quietness and wisdom when children are squabbling. It is this gift of peace that blesses our relationships.

Dear God, give me your peace in every part of today.

EP

God of peace

Blessed are the peacemakers, for they will be called children of God.

My husband and his sister were out walking one day. They stopped abruptly when they noticed what they were doing with their arms. They were both swinging and clapping their hands in front and behind their bodies as they strolled—they were identical in this behaviour. In horror and humour, they said, 'That's exactly what Mum did with her arms when she walked!' It was not a trait they wanted to immortalize.

Have you ever found yourself doing things just like your mum or just like your Aunt Mary? Sometimes that's good and sometimes it's dismaying, isn't it?

The phrase 'children of God' picks up this idea of being just like someone else—of imitating someone else. The phrase 'children of God' has the idea of being 'just like Mum', or in this verse 'just like God'. A 'chip off the old block', so to speak. When we are peacemakers we are being 'just like God' because peace-making is a God-like activity.

Peace-making is not the same as peace-loving. Peace-lovers often create more trouble by allowing a threatening or dangerous situation to develop. Or sometimes they compromise or passively accept wrong things and don't take action as they ought—just to keep the so-called peace.

Whatever, and wherever, our present war zones are, God clearly calls us to be peacemakers just as he is a peacemaker. On many occasions, my daughters have heard, 'You must be Elaine's daughter—you look just like her!' Wouldn't it be great to have people around us say, 'You must be God's daughter! You're just like him—you keep making peace!'

Dear God, help us to be just like you in our world—to be peacemakers this day.

EP

God of peace

For he [Jesus] himself is our peace, who has made the two one and has destroyed the barrier, the dividing wall of hostility… He came and preached peace to you who were far away and peace to those who are near.

Within ten minutes in my office, the couple I was counselling were arguing rather noisily with one another, each vigorously defending his and her position. They both had good reason for their hurt and their anger. There was a long litany of broken promises, hurtful words and accusations, and of neglect and disrespect—none of which the other had intentionally inflicted on the other.

Both of them wanted their marriage to last and work but their history of hurt and hurting had become a habitual way of responding. The dividing wall of hostility was clearly evident. My task was to broker peace by somehow standing in the middle of their angry words and raw emotion, to dismantle the wall of hostility brick by brick, and to rebuild a house of peace.

Sometimes peace-making means *being peace* for others, just as Jesus is our peace. I think one of the difficulties of being peace for others, or being a peacemaker, is that peacemakers regularly get crucified. It is a fairly risky business. But risky or not, Jesus calls us not only to bring peace into our fragmented, warring, broken world, but also to make peace where we are.

Lord, make me an instrument of your peace; where there is hatred let me sow love; where there is injury pardon… for it is in giving that we receive; it is in pardoning that we are pardoned; it is in dying that we are born again to eternal life.

FRANCIS OF ASSISI

EP

God of plans

'For I know the plans I have for you,' declares the Lord, 'plans to prosper you and not to harm you, plans to give you hope and a future.'

As we near the end of the millennium, what hope and encouragement do you have? What sense of a future?

I remember the day when my husband was diagnosed with cancer. It sent shock waves reverberating throughout my being. What if he dies? What will I do? Where will I live? Fear coiled its grip around my heart. It felt like life was out of control. I felt helpless and trapped. Without hope, without a future.

This text in Jeremiah comes to the children of Israel when they are in captivity in Babylon—facing seventy years in that foreign place. God said, 'Settle down in this place, seek peace and prosperity for the city of Babylon, because if it prospers you too will prosper.' And, indeed, prosperity did come for captive Israel in that foreign land.

Sometimes I feel like a captive in a world gone crazy! But in the middle of our out-of-control world, God has plans for you and for me: plans to prosper you and not to harm you, plans to give you hope and a future.

As my husband and I faced cancer and the ensuing treatment together, our values, our focus and our priorities were all challenged. Our faith grew to a new depth, to a greater clarity and power—all because the diagnosis of cancer forced us to re-evaluate everything. We 'settled down and sought peace' in the middle of cancer. It was there, in the middle, that we found God gave us hope and a future.

Thank you, Jesus, that you are a God of plans, of hope and of a future.

EP

God of plans

*'Then you will call upon me and come and pray to me, and I
will listen to you. You will seek me and find me when you seek
me with all your heart. I will be found by you,' declares the
Lord, 'and will bring you back from captivity.'*

She is a dear and trusted friend. When I need to dump stuff,
she's there to receive and listen. She sifts and sorts things I say,
disregards the impulsive, challenges the questionable, and
affirms the good. She rejoices with my joys and is sad with my
hurts. I feel safe in being with her. She remembers things that are
happening in my life. She is a wonderful gift to me.

I get the sense that these verses in Jeremiah are about God's
desire to have a similar relationship with us. He has already told
us that he has plans to prosper and not harm us, plans to give
hope and a future. He really is there rooting for us!

But we need to seek him out—genuinely! Not in some stuffy
religious way but in a dynamic and deep way. He wants to be
found by you and by me. He wants to rescue us from our captivities of hurt and fear and abandonment. But we must seek him
with our whole heart, not just a corner of it. Then we will find
and be found.

I sometimes wonder if it actually takes the seriousness of captivity before we are desperate enough to seek God with our
whole heart. What a frightening thought!

*God of hope, give us wisdom and determination to seek you with our
whole heart—right now in this situation—until we find you. Bring us
back from our captivities.*

EP

God of plans

You intended to harm me, but God intended it for good to accomplish what is now being done, the saving of many lives.

Talk about a dysfunctional family and vicious sibling rivalry! The sons of Jacob, the siblings of Joseph, take the cake! Older sons and brothers who so hate their younger seventeen-year-old brother, Joseph, that they sell him into slavery in a foreign country.

Joseph's life definitely took some interesting turns: a slave in charge of his Egyptian master's household, the 'well-built and handsome' object of a woman's lust, a prisoner falsely accused of improper sexual conduct, an interpreter of Pharaoh's dreams, the second-in-command of all of Egypt.

Do you get a sense of the strange complexity of Joseph's life? A series of surprising turns seemingly triggered by his brothers' hatred and jealousy. I wonder if you relate to such strange turns in your own life's journey.

As I have been reflecting on Joseph's life I have been reflecting on my own life—and its surprising turns. As I careen almost out of control, around yet another sharp curve, it's fairly difficult to see God's intentions in this one.

As Joseph sat for thirteen years in prison, I wonder if he had similar thoughts? I wonder if you too are careening around yet another sharp curve wondering where God is.

Is it really possible that God intends all these careening turns for good? Can we *really* trust that God has plans for good for us? Can we trust him with our lives? Joseph did and look where he ended up.

God, give us faith to trust you as we hang on around yet another sharp curve in our journey.

EP

God of plans

You intended to harm me, but God intended it for good to accomplish what is now being done, the saving of many lives.

I don't know about you, but I find it very difficult to genuinely forgive those who intentionally hurt me and add to the unhappily surprising turns in my life. My feelings of anger and injustice and just plain wrong are so strong within me. I usually want vengeance and I often want it exacted publicly!

So when I read of Joseph's generous and kind response to his brothers in Genesis 50, I am intrigued and baffled and humbled. You see, I kind of want the brothers to get smushed! Now, I'd really like to be as generous as Joseph, but forgiving thirteen years in prison and slavery—I don't know! I think our natural tendency is revenge, and our natural fear is like that of the brothers—that Joseph will hold a grudge and pay them back for all the wrong.

Joseph's generous forgiveness is quite simply unnatural! Because it is so like God—unlike human behaviour! It is as if those thirteen years in prison made him unnaturally godly rather than naturally vengeful. Even if God's sovereign intentions are for good outcomes, I would like to think that we could develop this God-likeness without thirteen years of imprisonment.

Perhaps if we look closely at our own circumstances we can see God working actively for our good right now, here in our own sharp turns—especially in those places where others are intentionally harming us.

Dear God, please find us in those places where others are intending to harm us and bring good in those places. Transform us into generous, kind people in a world that is often unjust and cruel.

EP

Joshua—servant

The Lord would speak to Moses face to face, as a man speaks with his friend. Then Moses would return to the camp, but his young assistant Joshua son of Nun did not leave the tent.

I remember singing 'Joshua fit de battle of Jericho' at school, and I suspect that images of tumbling walls spring to mind for others too whenever Joshua is mentioned. The conquering of the walled city of Jericho by unorthodox methods is probably Joshua's most famous achievement. But it was not where he started.

Joshua. A popular contemporary name and his own book in the Bible. I confess, he has always fascinated me. As I am delving into the eventful history of Old Testament Israel, I am beginning to discover why. Why not risk a spin into days BC, and experience the drama? Here we are, in the middle of the wilderness, thousands of Israelites having escaped from the slavery of tyrannical Egypt. About 1400BC. The great Moses is struggling to lead an alternately obedient and rebellious crowd through a hostile landscape to a new land. They are nomads with only the promise of a future. Their existence is hand to mouth and their journey perilous. They are glad to be free until something goes wrong, and then they want to go back. They have not got the hang of trusting God, nor supporting Moses.

But Hoshea was different. Moses chose him for his assistant and renamed him Joshua, meaning 'the Lord saves' (Numbers 13:16). What did he see in him? Moses took him up the mountain, the one no one else dared set foot on (Exodus 24:13). He put him in charge of the 'tent of meeting', where Moses spoke to God. He trusted Joshua as a man of integrity who was willing to serve and to learn. Most of all, he must have sensed in him a kindred spirit, a heart that responded to the call of God above all else.

If Moses was your boss, what would he sense in you?
Read Philippians 1:4.

                                                                    DA

Joshua—action man

*So Joshua fought the Amalekites as Moses had ordered, and
Moses, Aaron and Hur went to the top of the hill. As long as
Moses held up his hands, the Israelites were winning, but
whenever he lowered his hands the Amalekites were winning.*

This is Joshua's first real battle. He had trained as Moses' assistant, and been swept up into the high drama of the escape of an
entire nation from the oppressive Egyptian regime. He saw
Moses stretch out his hand over the Red Sea and watched as
strong winds drove the water back for them to cross over. As the
journey into the dry desert began, he too was soon gasping with
thirst. He was at Moses' side when he threw a stick into the
waters of Marah to sweeten them. Then there was no food.

His fellow travellers grumbled, and Joshua observed Moses
crying out to God on their behalf. He gathered the manna that
God provided and ate the quail.

Life in the desert had not been a picnic. Then a new threat
descended as the Amalekites attacked. For the first time, Joshua
was put in charge of the defending Israelite army. They won, but
only because Moses was constantly interceding to God on their
behalf. Joshua passed the test of military leadership, but his
prowess was tempered by obedience. It seems he had learnt the
lessons of the desert experiences well. Though he was entrusted
with the battle, his dependence was not on himself. This up-and-
coming action man had worked out where the real power came
from.

No wonder Moses picked him out. Instead of stumbling from
one answer to prayer to the next big grumble, Joshua was making connections. God was faithful. God was on their side.

Is this one of the fascinations of Joshua's character? It is such
a challenge. How easy to forget God's faithfulness in the past and
join the worriers. God may have helped before, but can he do it
again?

Dear Lord, give me a Joshua-like confidence in you. Amen
Read Matthew 28:20.

DA

Joshua—spy

*Joshua son of Nun and Caleb son of Jephunneh, who were
among those who had explored the land, tore their clothes and
said to the entire Israelite assembly, 'The land we passed
through and explored is exceedingly good. If the Lord is pleased
with us, he will lead us into that land… Only do not rebel
against the Lord.'*

We have skipped on a bit here. The Israelites have arrived at the
edge of Canaan after further faith-stretching adventures in the
desert, including the reception of the Ten Commandments and
detailed instructions for their new community life (Exodus and
Leviticus). Disobedience to God has brought death (Leviticus
10:1–2), but the covenant relationship with their holy God has
been confirmed (Exodus 24), and they know they are special.

Now the journey is over and they face their promised land. It
is a beautiful place 'flowing with milk and honey' (v. 8). They
have experienced so much of God's faithfulness, yet now, right
on the edge of the promise, they chicken out. It is too scary.
Incredibly, the general panic is such that they even want to go
back to Egypt (v. 4). They block their ears to Joshua's encouragement and suggest stoning him. Joshua and Caleb are horrified. Their faith that God would do what he promised is
absolute. God said it, so they believed it. They faced death for
these convictions but their passionate faith did not waver.

This is stirring stuff. If I, if you, had been there, whose side
would we have joined? What similar heart-stopping challenges
to faith are you facing in your journey with God? Can you, with
Joshua, stand on God's promises and know that God's 'yes'
means 'yes'? His love for you, his care of your life, his presence
with you… can you depend on them like Joshua? The Israelites
were banished back into the desert for their unbelief. Apart from
our heroes, the adult generation never saw their promised land.
They missed out.

Lord, I gasp for that gift of faith I need from you. Help me to receive it.
DA

Joshua—the takeover

Now Joshua son of Nun was filled with the spirit of wisdom because Moses had laid his hands on him. So the Israelites listened to him and did what the Lord had commanded Moses.

There are times when someone's emerging leadership qualities are hard to miss, and so it was with Joshua. He was the natural choice to succeed Moses. How he and Caleb must have felt traipsing around the desert for an extra forty years one can only imagine. Certainly he would have taken on the mantle of leadership with no illusions as to the character of his fellow Israelites. Yet time and time again he had seen Moses plead with God to have mercy on his wayward people, so perhaps he had picked up his master's compassion and long-suffering. Joshua took on the challenge with his eyes open.

Did Joshua relish the prospect of leadership? Or did he shoulder it with a sigh? It is all too easy to take on a new project or responsibility with a welter of emotions and motives. Perhaps especially if it is 'for God' or 'the church'. It is so simple to get trapped into sorting something—or someone—out and think we are doing God a favour. At the other extreme, we can feel so insecure in our capabilities that a small task calls out gigantic anxieties in us.

Joshua was not in any of these tangles. He had long ago worked out that obedience to God's will was the only thing that mattered, and the only way to make a lasting difference in life. So he submitted himself to the imparting hands of Moses and received God's equipping. Don't rush ahead without God's strength or forget it is available to calm fear and worry. We may not be asked to lead a nation today, but everything counts. Let God equip you too.

Sometimes it is hard to receive. Why not ask a friend to lay hands on you for strength as Moses did with Joshua?

DA

Joshua—go for it!

As I was with Moses, so I will be with you; I will never leave you or forsake you. Be strong and courageous, because you will lead these people to inherit the land I swore to their forefathers to give them.

God is as good as his word. No sooner had Moses died and Joshua assumed leadership, than there was evidence of God's anointing and equipping. As God had spoken to and directed Moses, so now he related to Joshua. In this initial commissioning, God repeats four times the exhortation to be 'strong', 'courageous' and not 'discouraged'. He knew the testing days that lay ahead for Israel's new commander. But this was not an encouragement to a Rambo-like, jaw-setting kind of courage, despite Joshua's military expertise. There was only one reason for Joshua to face the future with confidence, and it was the one Joshua already knew: 'for the Lord your God will be with you wherever you go.' This, along with Joshua's obedience to God's law and commands, was all he needed.

It seems that Joshua made these principles the bedrock of his life. Not that he knew everything from now on, because there were lessons still waiting for him, but his courage in the face of fear, and his unshakeable faith in God's activity stand out as hallmarks of his lifestyle. He did it all the time. He made the straightforward connection between God's words and his life and got on with it.

I confess that I find this so challenging. I get caught in doubts and prevaricating, especially when surrounding circumstances seem to militate against God's involvement or even his presence sometimes. So often it seems that there is no evidence of divine activity or care except what God's word says. The promised land becomes only a promise and I cannot see a way in.

And yet. Isn't that precisely the situation Joshua was in?

Father—Joshua did it. I see others doing it.
I have even done it myself in the past.
But—help me to trust you today.

DA

Joshua—leader

*This is how you will know that the living God is among you
and that he will certainly drive out before you the Canaanites…
As soon as the priests who carry the ark of the Lord—the Lord
of all the earth—set foot in the Jordan, its waters flowing
downstream will be cut off and stand up in a heap.*

Just in case there were any Israelite doubts about Joshua's cre-
dentials for leadership, the big push into Canaanite territory
begins with divine intervention reminiscent of the Red Sea
crossing many years ago. This time it is the Jordan, and this second Israelite arrival on the edge of the promised land was pref-
aced by a more positive spy report than the previous one.

The spies—Joshua only sent two, no doubt carefully chosen
—reported that 'all the people are melting in fear because of us'
(2:24). There is no trace among the Israelites of the former
reluctance to take up their inheritance. Are these offspring of
the former generation made of sterner stuff? Or have they learnt
from their parents' disobedience? Whatever the reason, they follow God, represented by the ark of the Lord, willingly across the
newly dried-up river. It is not coincidental that the ark goes first.
It is God who is claiming the land for his chosen people. It is
God's battle. He is proclaiming his rightful lordship over the
land, the people and their gods.

Perhaps Israel had learnt some lessons in the previous forty
years. Perhaps Joshua had influenced them with his profound
understanding of the relationship between God's power and
human activity. 'Obedience to God' sounds so easy but I think it
is a learned art—to know when to act, when to wait; when to
speak, when to hold back; how to be sensitive to what God is
doing.

Joshua was good at listening to God and that has to be where
it starts.

The Lord will fight for you (Exodus 14:14).
*Read Joshua 4. Do you have memorials in your life to remind you of
God's goodness?*

DA

Joshua—tough obedience

At that time the Lord said to Joshua, 'Make flint knives and circumcise the Israelites again.' So Joshua made flint knives and circumcised the Israelites at Gibeath Haaraloth.

Do you ever find that great highs are followed by difficult lows? You come to a revelatory understanding, have a wonderful experience of God, or a big answer to prayer and then along comes the unwelcome intruder of pain or problems. 'It was all going so well…' you cry.

Think of the Israelites. Great stuff, this crossing the Jordan. Stepping out to claim a forty-year delayed promise, and beginning with a miracle, no less. What height will Joshua and God lead them to next? What? We have to be circumcised? You must be joking. We are ready for war, not weakness!

But God says, 'No, you are not prepared. You are my people and must be set aside for me. You can only do this in my strength.' The Israelites were touched by God in the most delicate area possible and rendered literally defenceless for a while. All the would-be warriors were thus consecrated to God before they lifted a sword. Their circumcised vulnerability reminded them painfully of their utter dependence on God.

Gibeath Haaraloth actually means 'hill of foreskins', which is a ghastly thought. But it was God's command, and he does not shirk the difficult areas of life, much as we would like him to. In revealing the Israelite nation's frailty, God drew them closer to himself, and reidentified them as his people. They were marked for life. This is the potential of those confusingly bleak times in our lives. They can draw us back to the true security and love that come only from intimacy with God.

Frail children of dust, and feeble as frail,
In thee do we trust, nor find thee to fail:
Thy mercies, how tender, how firm to the end,
Our maker, defender, redeemer and friend!
R. GRANT (1729–1838)

Read Joshua 5:13–15.

DA

Jericho day

*When the trumpets sounded, the people shouted, and at the
sound of the trumpet, when the people gave a loud shout, the
wall collapsed; so every man charged straight in, and they took
the city.*

And then there was Jericho. It is hard to imagine a crazier sce-
nario for battle than the entire Israelite army marching day after
day around a walled city in total silence. Just the chink of metal,
the squeak of leather and the tramp of feet would have reached
the ears of the defenders. Perhaps the ark of the Lord would have
flashed in the sunlight as the Canaanites peered over the battle-
ments and worried about the Israelite God. Day after day.

Sometimes obedience to God is like that. Just walking, faithfully, day after day. Like us, the Israelites had only the promise of
future victory to cling to as they traipsed on. Did they wonder if
it was worth it? Did it seem as ridiculous as following Christ can
seem, at those times when faith looks absurd, and trust outra-
geous? Yet they kept on, drawn by Joshua to go God's way. What
else could they do? They had crossed the Jordan, been circumcised, and the miraculous manna had ceased. They were committed now.

It is the same for us. No matter how crazy it may feel at times,
we are on the journey. We must go on. Now we know Jesus, there
is no turning back to the old ways. We cannot pretend he is not
there. (Or if we do, it does not work. I have tried it.) There is no
other course now, despite how upside-down life can be.

Joshua and the Israelites had their seventh day. The moment
when battle cries were released in a mighty shout and the walls
crumbled. Rahab and her family, who had protected Joshua's
spies, were spared, but the rest of the inhabitants destroyed.

Israel had taken her first city. Joshua's obedience and faith
were vindicated.

*Lord, give me the vision and courage to keep walking towards your
victory. Amen*
Read John 6:66–69.

DA

Reckoning day

Consecrate yourselves in preparation for tomorrow; for this is what the Lord, the God of Israel says: That which is devoted is among you, O Israel. You cannot stand against your enemies until you remove it.

A bit of background: Jericho was captured, but one man Achan took plunder, disobedient to the command that everything was 'devoted' to God, that is, either destroyed or put in God's treasury. Consequently, when a small Israelite army confidently attacked the town of Ai, it was completely routed.

Joshua was devastated. On his face before God, he learnt of Israel's sin. Joshua's battles were not for personal gain, but for God's glory. His trust in God's provision was such that he had willingly kept the 'devoted' ban to the letter, and not kept any booty. Here he had a fellow countryman who had disobeyed and brought judgment on them all. Joshua already knew that God took his own laws seriously. He had seen Moses' anger and frustration at Israel's waywardness and witnessed the punishments (e.g. Exodus 32). Gently he admonished Achan, calling him 'my son' (v. 19), but knowing he faced death for his misdeeds. Only after confession and punishment could Joshua confidently lead Israel to victory over Ai (ch. 8).

We may not like the raw nature of these life and death issues, but the principle of the dire consequences of sin is undeniable. Thinking we can get away with it is just foolishness. Wrongdoing affects not only us but also the community we live in. It cannot be ignored. If it is not dealt with, it will continue in its effect. Others will suffer too, no matter how much we like to pretend our lives are just a private matter between us and God. This was a painful episode for Joshua. Thankfully, we have Jesus to turn to when we foul things up, in a way Joshua never did. So don't hide like Achan. Confess and receive that liberating, hard-won forgiveness.

What would have happened to Israel if Achan and his sin had not been dealt with?
Read Joshua 8:1–29.

DA

God first

*Then Joshua built on Mount Ebal an altar to the Lord…
There, in the presence of the Israelites, Joshua copied on stones
the law of Moses, which he had written… Afterwards, Joshua
read all the words of the law.*

After all the agony of Achan's sin and then the thrill of military
victory over Ai, you might have expected Joshua to be yearning
for his next battle. I think I would have been. 'Aha. Got the hang
of it now. Keep right with God; utter obedience; go for it!' But
no. Joshua reins in the momentum and gathers the Israelite
nation for a ceremony. There were no war dances, no victory
celebrations, but instead a quiet, powerful renewal of their
covenant with God.

Imagine the scene: The Israelites assembled by Mount Ebal, a
myriad dark eyes watching as smoke curled up from the sacrifices. The altar, built of uncut stones, and the ark of the covenant
carried on the priests' shoulders. Then a hush descended as
Joshua read to them the laws which set them apart from the surrounding nations and sealed their relationship with God.

Thus their evolving national identity in a new land was
defined. Despite Joshua's brilliant military strategy in taking Ai,
he knew he owed its success to God. Only in deference to God
did it make any sense. They were not just another marauding
army. God was keeping promises, and they were part of something bigger. Joshua seems to have been acutely conscious of this
divine dynamic. He never forgot who was ultimately in charge.

In the comparatively humdrum—yet none the less real—battles of my daily life, I find it distressingly easy to lose precisely
that 'Joshua perspective'. Events and emotions turn a few cart-
wheels and leave me struggling to remember who is running the
show.

*The altar on Mount Ebal became the centre of worship for Israel in
the ensuing years. Where do you go to renew your relationship with
God?*
Read Psalm 47.

DA

Deception

When the people of Gibeon heard what Joshua had done to Jericho and Ai, they resorted to a ruse: They went as a delegation whose donkeys were loaded with worn-out sacks and old wineskins, cracked and mended.

Well, you can understand it. The Gibeonites did not want to be killed and ransacked. So they pretended to be from a far-off country that offered no threat to invading Israel, and wangled a treaty out of Joshua. Caught off guard, the men of Israel 'did not enquire of the Lord' (v. 14) and discovered three days later that they had guaranteed peace to a near neighbour.

So for all his military brilliance and faithfulness to God, Joshua was deceived. He must have been so angry—perhaps most of all with himself. It is not a nice feeling to be tricked. Often, like Joshua, it comes to light too late to change the consequences. But at least he did not wallow in self-recrimination. He hauled the Gibeonites before him and challenged them with their trickery. He behaved honourably in that he spared their lives as promised, but made reparation to his countrymen in assigning the Gibeonites to menial labour (vv. 23–27).

Perhaps Joshua was so geared up for battle he was not ready for this more subtle attack. But he did try to make amends, and his treaty eventually led to victories over other countries. We too can read situations wrongly and draw erroneous conclusions. It can be plain embarrassing or it can be positively dangerous. We are all open to deception. People do desperate things for desperate reasons, and sometimes only God knows the truth. I had a friend once who convinced us she was terminally ill. She wasn't. It caused a double agony all round, and I still wonder if I had stopped to really 'enquire of the Lord' whether things could have been different.

But if the mighty Joshua could be fooled and consequently create a muddle—be encouraged! We are human too. At least the fate of the Israelite nation does not rest on our shoulders.

Read Romans 8:28.

DA

The conqueror

Joshua took all these royal cities and their kings and put them to the sword… The Israelites carried off for themselves all the plunder and livestock of these cities, but all the people they put to the sword until they completely destroyed them, not sparing anyone that breathed.

After the embarrassment of the Gibeonite debacle, Joshua went on to lead the Israelite army to unquestionable victories. The attacking force defeated king after king, and conquered land for Israel in the Southern and Northern Kingdoms. Chapter 12 of Joshua records an impressive list of beaten monarchs, all falling victim to Joshua's battle cry, 'Do not be afraid; do not be discouraged. Be strong and courageous' (v. 25). Thus Joshua constantly encouraged the Israelites with the commissioning words God had given to him.

Yet what of the slaughtered Canaanites? They stood condemned by God for their pagan ways (Genesis 15:16), but the thought of God commanding their unrelenting massacre is hard to take. Especially when you think of the children. There are no satisfying answers to this—I have delved into many commentaries. But it has to be said that Joshua knew Israel would come under the same punishment if it disobeyed God (Joshua 23:12–13), and also that Joshua was never given *carte blanche* to conquer the world. His was a particular, limited task—to find the people of God a land.

Perhaps this is where Joshua's utter loyalty to God gets its cutting edge. Because he was doing it God's way, in God's strength, it was not only successful, but also meaningful. This was part of God's larger unfolding story of redemption, not just a military take-over. The bloody side is horrible, but throughout there are the threads of punishment and grace, laws and love, which teach us about God. We can look back on it all and learn.

We may struggle with the gore and debate it, but the question is: will we do life God's way, no matter what it takes?

Lord, help me to face the difficult areas. Amen

                                                                        DA

True success

When they had finished dividing the land into its allotted portions, the Israelites gave Joshua son of Nun an inheritance among them, as the Lord had commanded.

If geography is your thing, it is worth ploughing through Joshua chapters 13 to 19 to trace the detailed descriptions of the conquered Canaanite land as it was parcelled out to the Israelite tribes. The account opens with Caleb's allotment and finishes with Joshua's. This seems very fitting, as they were the only spies of the original twelve to have seen the land's potential. It is also notable that Joshua, true to form, left his claim till the end, and in no sense attempted to lord it over anyone. He knew his place. He had fulfilled his mission. He could look back with satisfaction at having done his bit.

However, this was with the awareness that there was more land to be taken (13:1). It seems that his years in the Lord's service had taught Joshua well that God knew what he was doing. He could leave the continuation of the story with him.

This man just goes on being challenging, doesn't he? How often have you been anxious to cross every 't' and dot every 'i' in case God forgets? Don't you ever get tempted to fix everything for everybody, rather than leaving it to the Almighty? Or even to someone else?

Take a leaf out of Joshua's book. He knew what he was supposed to do and he did that and no more. He was not tempted to 'just one more battle'. He did not move unless God said so. Oh for his wisdom and sensitivity to God's spirit!

Lord, now lettest thou thy servant depart in peace
according to thy word.
For mine eyes have seen thy salvation,
Which thou hast prepared before the face of all people;
A light to lighten the Gentiles, and the glory of thy people Israel.
LUKE 2:29–32 (AV)

DA

A promise kept

If serving the Lord seems undesirable to you, then choose for yourselves this day whom you will serve, whether the gods your forefathers served beyond the River, or the gods of the Amorites, in whose land you are living. But as for me and my household, we will serve the Lord.

At the grand age of one hundred and ten, Joshua died. His last act as leader of the Israelites was to renew their covenant with God. He reminded them of their history, laid out the choice, and inspired them to pledge allegiance once again to their God. Here we see the hallmark of his life—he did not wait to see what his fellow countrymen will do, but blazed a trail of obedience straight towards God.

Throughout Joshua's adventurous life, he and God had been faithful to each other; and it had worked. Joshua saw victories, he knew dependence, he learned hard lessons, but always he did it God's way. He was bold and courageous for God and it paid off.

As we come to the end of our brief visit into Joshua's life, let his consistent example inspire you. Joshua faced incredible odds, and without God's help he would surely have failed. But because God was *with* him, he had the courage to attempt great things.

The same is true for us. God has promised in Jesus never to leave us, or forsake us (Matthew 28:20). He will never abandon us to the mercy of circumstance. He will always be with us and he will always be for us (Romans 8:31). He will equip us as surely as he did Joshua (Philippians 4:13). He will guide us as he did him (John 16:13).

Why not take a look at the hindrances to trusting God that would send you scuttering back into the wilderness? Should they be allowed to hold you back? Wouldn't it be better to leave the doubts behind and make the choice with Joshua today to go for the promised land, no matter what it takes?

Only: be strong and very courageous.

DA

Millennium promises

Arise, shine, for your light has come, and the glory of the Lord rises upon you.

When my neighbour's third child was born, one of her toddlers, watching his sister in the bath, asked in a puzzled way, 'But what's Amanda for?' We can all sometimes wonder why we dig gardens, paint walls, take photographs, worry about buying presents, when we are all going to die and someone else is going to throw the photographs away and dig up our plants. Somehow we need to know what we are for, and part of that is to know what is going to happen to us all in the end.

Over the next two weeks we are going to be reading from the last chapters of Isaiah in the Old Testament, and from Revelation, the very last book of the New Testament. In these chapters we are given a vision, a picture of the future, a promise that one day we will know all the answers, that we will discover what our lives were for.

We begin with a rousing call that sounds a bit like the bugle waking campers as the dawn breaks in the eastern sky. The Lord is calling his people to wake up because a wonderful day is beginning.

Can you remember waiting for something wonderful to happen? I can still just about remember the feelings I had when, as a child, I went to bed on Christmas Eve, knowing that the next morning there would be a knobbly sock and a pile of wrapped presents by my bed. 'Arise, shine,' the Lord says. The moment you have been waiting for has come.

Wake me up, Lord; show me as I read these verses that you have promised a wonderful future for those who follow you, and may that promise give a rosy tint to all I do.

MK

Big promises

No longer will violence be heard in your land, nor ruin or
destruction within your borders, but you will call your walls
Salvation and your gates Praise.

Many people are waiting for the start of the millennium. The
digital clocks are clicking forward to a big party. I expect by 6
January 2000, when we all go back to work, a lot of people will
be wondering why they were so excited. It would be different if
we thought the millennium was bringing an end to violence!

The Lord's words here are being spoken to 'Jerusalem', to his
chosen people, in their city, where the Lord was worshipped in
his temple. Only things had not turned out too well. Jerusalem
had been conquered by foreign armies, its people exiled; the
temple knocked down. But even before that, the people had
stopped praising the Lord, and had disobeyed his laws. The
prophets told them that they had brought ruin and destruction
on themselves.

But now the Lord promises a wonderful restoration—no more
violence, no more tears, but rebuilding, a new start, a glorious
dawn with every hope fulfilled. Some people are desperately
hoping that the millennium will bring a new start for our world.

Imagine reading these words today on the morning after your
church has been burnt down and Christian friends attacked,
beaten and killed, in Sudan, in Indonesia, in northern Nigeria.
Do these promises mean anything now in today's world?

As we read on we will begin to see that the Lord fulfils his
promises in two ways. As we trust in him, we see them being fulfilled partly here and now. (Jerusalem's temple was rebuilt. Later
it was demolished again.) But the final and tremendous fulfilment is still ahead of us, when the day of the Lord comes at last.

Pray for those Christians who live in violent parts of our world, that
they will be able to put their trust in these promises today, even though
they have to wait for them to come true tomorrow.

                                                              MK

Fulfilment in Jesus

The Spirit of the Sovereign Lord is on me, because the Lord has anointed me to preach good news to the poor. He has sent me to bind up the broken-hearted, to proclaim freedom for the captives and release from darkness for the prisoners.

Most people long for freedom for captives, gladness instead of mourning, praise instead of despair. Isaiah says that there is someone who can bring this new life, new joy and new start, someone with the Spirit of the Lord in him.

We can imagine the shock and surprise in the synagogue at Nazareth around 2000 years ago when Jesus read these verses and then said, 'Today this scripture is fulfilled in your hearing' (Luke 4:18–21). Jesus claimed that he is the one who fulfils all these great promises of God we have been reading about. He is the new dawn—the wonderful Christmas morning present.

The most important moment in history when God begins to save us and restore us, does not come with great armies but with a man who lives and dies on earth. So the fulfilment of God's promises of enormous light and glory begin with a small vulnerable human baby. His death brings forgiveness, new life, and the promise of a wonderful future. And the first sign that this has begun is that he came back from death.

What are our longings for a new year, a new century, a new millennium? Relationships we long to see on a better footing? Healing for people we love who are unhappy or hurt? Putting right damage we have done or has been done to us? As you pray, bring these to Jesus, sent to bind up the broken-hearted.

Perhaps we will see these prayers answered soon, but we may have to wait, seeing them partly answered now. Write down all you have prayed for and keep watch. We are sometimes too preoccupied to notice that there are some answers now, even if we have to go on waiting for the final wonderful dawn.

MK

The marriage we were made for

As a bridegroom rejoices over his bride, so will your God rejoice over you.

Running through the Bible in the Old and New Testaments there is a lovely series of pictures that describes the relationship between the Lord and us as a marriage, a covenant of love. It can be very powerful and very physical. There is a dark side as God mourns over his people's betrayal of love, calling it adultery. Here in this passage the message is that we are wooed, loved and chosen just as a lover chooses his bride. We are clothed in bridal dress, wearing a royal diadem (v. 3). Our (single) name is changed, from Desolate and Deserted, to My Delight is in Her, and Married (v. 4, NRSV). Remember that Jesus, too, talked of himself as the bridegroom (Mark 2:19–20). Like an engagement, this relationship can start for us now if we turn in love to our Lord. But the final wedding feast will come when heaven opens for us and all the promises of our betrothal are fulfilled.

The Lord speaks of his relationship to his people as the deep, passionate, committed love of a husband in the best possible marriage. Some of us have known such love for a time; others have glimpsed what it could be, but sadly have never found it, or have lost it far too soon. But the Lord is our lover now and for ever and we can look forward with total certainty to all the rich fulfilment of the wedding feast one day.

Lord, help me to remember I am chosen, loved and cherished by you—today, tomorrow and for ever.

MK

I won't let it happen again

Never again will I give your grain as food for your enemies, and never again will foreigners drink the new wine for which you have toiled; but those who harvest it will eat it and praise the Lord.

'I have worked so hard to make this business really successful and now in one week it's been taken over, and I've been made redundant.'

'I did my very best for my son, and now he's dropped out of college, gone to Nepal and doesn't even phone us any more.'

Working very hard at something and having it snatched away happens to lots of people—to farmers whose crops fail, to those whose health fails when they are still young, to refugees who have to leave everything behind. Because we live in a fallen and unfair world these things will happen and not just to those who deserve it. But God says, 'I will put it right.' 'Your Saviour will come and he brings reward and recompense' (v. 11).

Injustice, disappointment and unfairness are hard to bear and sometimes the resulting bitterness and resentment can eat us up. We need to hold on to the promises of God that he knows what has happened to us and will certainly put it right one day. 'Never again' is his promise to us. Jesus tasted defeat, betrayal and injustice and knows what they are like. He doesn't say they won't happen, but he does promise that we will one day hear heaven shout, 'Never again.' 'Never again' is the message of the resurrection.

Sometimes we need help to begin to forgive those who have hurt us, and to let go of resentment and the desire to pay them back. We may need someone we can trust to help us bring it all to the Lord. 'Father, forgive them. They don't know what they are doing,' Jesus prayed. Are we able to pray that?

MK

Waiting for the great day

No eye has seen any God besides you, who acts on behalf of those who wait for him.

However busy we are with a very full life, when we know that something wonderful is going to happen, we are also waiting. We wait for a holiday, a visit, an appointment. We wait for the millennium, for Christmas morning, for our wedding day. We wait for someone we love to come home after a long time away. We may be waiting, and worrying that it might not happen. Sometimes we can be very impatient, like children who want his presents *now*, and cannot wait for Christmas morning. God's promises come but we have to wait for them.

In these verses the people of God are being impatient. They cannot wait for the promised dawn when everything will be put right, the presents opened and the feast begun. 'Why don't you come? Why do we have to wait?' Then they answer this question for themselves. 'You have hidden your face from us and made us waste away because of our sins' (v. 7). Why do they have to wait? Because they have turned away from God. He is not teasing by promising presents that he then keeps hidden. He is waiting for us to ask for them—to admit that we have been wrong and to ask for his forgiveness.

These great promises are not for those who do no wrong; they are for those who have done wrong and have been forgiven. The Saviour who died for us and came alive again, brings the fulfilment of God's promises to us, by making our forgiveness possible, so that we can wait knowing the promises are for us.

So we wait, Lord, loved and forgiven and doing right, with these wonderful promises about to come true. Lord, give me a sense of your glory just round the corner so that waiting for your coming brings colour and excitement to all I do.

MK

A new heaven and a new earth

*Behold I will create new heavens and a new earth. The former
things will not be remembered, nor will they come to mind...
the sound of weeping and of crying will be heard in it no more.*

In our last verse from Isaiah, the Lord promises us not just heaven, *but a new earth.*

All the delights of the world around us will be restored and
recreated—sunsets and rainbows, roses and redwoods, mountains and hedgerows, human love and music, poetry and language—all this will be ours to enjoy, unspoilt. We live on a spoilt
earth, but God gives us enough glimpses of beauty to hint at
what the new earth will be like.

All the bad things will be gone and forgotten. No more sadness, resentment, pain, disablement, prejudice and cruelty. They
will not even be remembered. The 'never again' promise is
repeated. No babies that die, no building things up to see them
torn down, no planting crops that we do not harvest; no old people finishing their lives in misery. There will be no more damaged
earth; no more killing and hunting; even lions will eat straw
beside the ox.

We live in a world where bad and good are completely mixed
up together. Where good things that God gives us to enjoy are
spoilt. We paint in beautiful colours, but the paint flakes off. He
puts the beauty of gold and diamonds into the rocks, but humans
fight and kill to find them, and steal and cheat to possess them.

When we pray, 'Your will be done on earth as in heaven,' we
are promising to do all we can to put things right. Our work,
filled with his Spirit, is to make our earth more like his heaven
until he comes in glory to create new heavens and a new earth.

*Praise him for all the glimpses of heaven we have on earth, especially
as we worship our Lord Jesus who was made man on earth.*

MK

Heaven opens up to us

*Then I heard what sounded like a great multitude… shouting,
'Hallelujah! For our Lord God Almighty reigns. Let us rejoice
and be glad and give him glory! For the wedding of the Lamb
has come and his bride has made herself ready.'*

I am writing these words on a cold November day. The sky is
heavy and grey. The light is poor, even at midday. There is
enough rain in the air to chill the bones. The hills are dim grey
against the darker grey of the sky. The trees are dripping and life-
less. The world is muffled, colourless, cold and silent.

Imagine suddenly it all changing in a flash to blazing, tropical,
midday sunshine—and not just sudden light, warmth and colour,
but noise too. That is what John is describing. It is heaven open-
ing up.

We have read in Isaiah the promise of a future heaven for
those of us on earth. Here we glimpse heaven itself. We see the
shining, piercing light of the glory of God. When the Lord said
to his people, 'Arise, shine, your light has come,' this is where the
light came from.

Heaven is here and now, although we cannot see it at the
moment. The sun is the other side of the clouds. All its joy and
glory is real now, waiting for the right time to break through into
our world. The multitudes of heaven are shouting in a wonderful Hallelujah chorus, 'The wedding of the Lamb has come, and
his bride has made herself ready.' When he comes there will be
no more doubts. We will be there in the bright sunshine of heav-
en. It will be greater than anything we have ever known, but we
won't be in the back row craning to see; we are the guests at the
wedding, but we are also, as the Church, the bride, taking pride
of place next to the bridegroom.

*Help me to be ready for you when you come, Lord, as a bride for her
husband.*

MK

The warrior judge

I saw heaven standing open and there before me was a white horse, whose rider is called Faithful and True. With justice he judges and makes war... He is dressed in a robe dipped in blood, and his name is the Word of God.

Jesus the Lamb, whose wedding feast is prepared for his people, is also the warrior judge on a white horse, whose robe is dipped in blood. The word-pictures John draws are vivid and shocking, and sometimes not easy to understand. If you look back at Isaiah 63:1–6 you can see that John uses Isaiah's words to describe this new vision of God at work.

Jesus is King of kings and Lord of lords, bringing justice and judgment. He comes out of heaven followed by heavenly armies, to strike down the nations. This is the other side of God's promised 'Never again'. If all the bad things, the pain and suffering are to be ended, then the wicked have to be brought to justice. We cannot have the love of the Saviour without his justice.

Jean discovered that her twelve-year-old son, Hugh, was involved with a gang who were stealing from younger boys at school. When she confronted him he admitted what he had done, but Hugh was horrified when she took him to see the head. She agreed with the head about the punishment and made sure it was carried out. Hugh knew she loved him and for this reason he expected her to protect him from justice, not to help carry out the punishment. But true love does not let us get away with evil. If we do not seek the forgiveness of the Lord's love, then we will face the judgment of his love.

Lord, help me to be honest about myself and to accept your judgment on my life; to ask for your full and free forgiveness for all I have done wrong. Help me to put right any damage I have done to others, even if the consequences are hard to bear.

MK

The millennium again

He seized the dragon, that ancient serpent, who is the devil, or Satan, and bound him for a thousand years.

A friend was telling me that her son likes books about real things; about tractors and dinosaurs. He has little time for everyday stories, let alone fantasy and poetry! Like many of us he will probably find some parts of Revelation hard to cope with later on. It is full of descriptions that sound like fantasy and science fiction.

In today's passage, there are two difficult ideas. The first is the binding of the devil. John sees an angel coming down to earth and capturing Satan, using four different words to describe the power of evil in our world. The angel has a chain and a key to the prison and he locks the devil up. But for a limited time, not for ever.

God is teaching us two things here. First, evil is very powerful, and it takes a lot of holy strength to control it. Second, God is able to control the devil who is not free to do whatever he likes in our world. Throughout the ages human thinking has often fallen into the trap of neglecting one of these truths about evil, either underestimating its strength and power, or believing that Satan is God's equal in the struggle to control our world. On the cross God in Christ defeated evil once and for all, but it was a titanic battle.

The second picture is the thousand years—a millennium. Christians have wondered what this means, and some have thought that there will be literally a thousand years of human history when evil is under lock and key. But from what we know about the use of numbers in this book it is more likely to be a symbol than literally a thousand years, a symbol standing for God's perfect heavenly time. So John is letting us know that God is in control, that evil has limited powers, and his perfect heaven breaks through into our time-controlled world.

MK

The great white throne

And I saw the dead, great and small, standing before the throne, and books were opened. Another book was opened, which is the book of life.

The final day when God blazes in splendour like the sun, and everything is put right, may happen before the millennium or not for another thousand years. But John says that when that day comes we will all stand before the throne of God.

And then the books are opened! I would be very interested to know what is in the books about some people, but I am not so sure I want anyone else to know what is in mine! This is John's way of saying that God knows all that we have ever done. But there is another book—the book of life, which has the names of all those who will enter heaven. Their list of wrong-doings has been crossed out, wiped away by the mercy of the Saviour who died to cancel them.

But what of those who are not in the book of life? We may not want to face the last sentence of our reading, but people cannot turn their back on God and say no to him and expect him to drag them into heaven against their will. Some of my family do not believe in God. In ordinary daily life, telephone calls and meals together, it is hard to remember that heaven is just around the corner and that people I love will stand before the throne of God and may have to face the loss of heaven. I know that the Lord is calling me to pray for them, and to live so that they can see something of God in me.

Do you know that your name is in the book of life? If you have turned to Jesus, then it is. Make a commitment now to pray for someone who does not know him.

MK

A new heaven and a new earth

He will wipe every tear from their eyes. There will be no more death or mourning or crying or pain, for the old order of things has passed away.

Then I saw a new heaven and a new earth, John says, repeating the words we read in Isaiah some days ago. John is told to write down the vision as trustworthy and true. Because John did as he was told we can read these verses two thousand years later in English.

John tries to describe the new heaven and earth, but finding the words to do so is very hard. He is drawing a mind picture of something outside our experience and beyond our language. Like Isaiah, John talks of heaven as a new Jerusalem, but how do you describe a perfect city? He says the city is a perfect cube, over a thousand miles high, wide and deep. It is made of gold so pure it looks like glass, and precious stones with wonderful sparkling names—jasper, sapphire, emerald, carnelian, topaz, amethyst and pearl.

But the most wonderful thing is that at the centre of this imagined city there is a throne and round that throne multitudes are shouting and singing, but on the throne is a God who wipes away the tears from the eyes of any person who is crying! It is not like the great throne-rooms of this world's rulers, because the one on the throne is our Father, and beside him is the Son who bears the scars of our rescue.

Let him fill you with his joy and peace as he wipes away the tears from your eyes.

MK

Bringing heaven to earth

Then the angel showed me the river of the water of life, as clear as crystal, flowing from the throne of God and of the Lamb down the middle of the great street of the city.

When we see programmes or read about people who do not have access to clean water, then we begin to realize that water is far more precious than gold or silver. The lands of the Bible are places that know drought, when water is short and what is available may be badly polluted. No wonder John sees at the centre of the heavenly city a wonderful river of crystal-clear water.

A young couple from our church work for a water development project in Tanzania. They plan and engineer the bringing of water to villages and farms where up till now the women, mostly, have had to walk many miles to carry water back home. They are working to bring the kingdom of God on earth, to begin making God's promises for the future come true now. They are making these words of God real for Tanzanian villagers. They are saying that fresh water is part of God's heaven on earth!

All the promises we have read—comfort for pain, tears wiped away, captives freed, the broken-hearted bound up, as well as the shouting and singing in worship to God, the acceptance of his love and forgiveness—are promises that will fully come true only when God brings an end to human history and everyone will see him face to face. But they are also promises for now, in part and they can begin to come true now for you and the people round you. We can make a bit of heaven come on earth. That is the work of the disciples of Jesus Christ.

Help me to know your heaven so that I can start to make heaven on earth.

MK

Come, Lord Jesus

The Spirit and the bride say, 'Come!' And let him who hears say, 'Come!' Whoever is thirsty, let him come; and whoever wishes, let him take the free gift of the water of life.

Jesus says, 'Behold I am coming soon.' Come, Lord Jesus.

    Jesus says, 'I am the Alpha and the Omega, the First and the Last.' Come, Lord Jesus.

    Jesus says, 'I am the root and the offspring of David.' Come, Lord Jesus.

    Jesus says, 'I am the bright Morning Star.' Come, Lord Jesus.

and that will be heaven

and that will be heaven
at last   the first unclouded
seeing

      to stand like the sunflower
turned full face to the sun   drenched
with light   in the still centre
held   while the circling planets
hum with an utter joy

        seeing and knowing
at last   in every particle
seen and known   and not turning
away

   never turning away
again

EVANGELINE PATERSON

MK

Tell us when

When he was sitting on the Mount of Olives, the disciples came to him privately, saying, 'Tell us, when will this be, and what will be the sign of your coming and of the end of the age?'

The Mount of Olives is a low hill, opposite the 600-yard-long eastern wall of the courtyard that surrounded the temple. The courtyard is dominated now by the golden dome of a big mosque. But as Jesus and his friends sat on the hill, looking west across the valley, they gazed on the gilded Jewish temple whose rebuilding had started in 46BC and was still unfinished. Earlier in the day the disciples had drawn his attention to the building: 'Look, teacher, what massive stones! What magnificent buildings!' 'It will all be flattened,' was his reply.

So they asked, 'When is it all going to happen—the temple destroyed and the end of the age?' They could not envisage that this fine building, so solidly constructed, could be destroyed before the world ended. In fact, it was demolished forty years later, without even being completed. The disciples did not understand that they were asking about two events, not one. It is as if they were looking towards two ranges of mountains with a valley in between. From their perspective it looked like one range. But we live between the two events, and can look back to the destruction of Jerusalem by Titus' army in AD70 and forward to Jesus' return in… no one knows when. In this chapter Jesus' replies are intertwined.

This month before Christmas is known by the church as Advent, which means 'coming'. It is traditionally the time for looking forward to Jesus' second coming, but instead our preparations for celebrating his first coming predominate. So in the next two weeks we will use our readings (some of them difficult ones) to focus on his second advent even while we are busy preparing to remember his first advent.

Lord, I pray that my busyness this month may not override my desire to learn from you.

RG

Don't be deceived

*Jesus answered them, 'Beware that no one leads you astray.
For many will come in my name, saying "I am the Messiah!"
and will lead many astray.'*

These disciples! They had been so slow to learn, slow to trust,
slow to change. Jesus knew that they were vulnerable, so he
warned them of those who would come and claim to be the
Messiah. It has happened down the centuries; we have seen it
recently in Waco, Texas, in the community that blindly followed
the self-styled 'messiah' leader. Watch out, Jesus says, so that you
are not tricked. As he makes it plain later in this chapter, when
he comes again it will be unmistakable. He will not come again
as human, but will return as the king of glory.

Deceit turns many from the path of following God and his
truth. 'The serpent tricked me,' was Eve's self-defence for dis-
obeying God's clear command (Genesis 3:13). 'I urge you,' said
Paul, 'watch out for those who cause divisions and put obstacles
in your way that are contrary to the teaching you have heard…
By smooth talk and flattery…' (how like the serpent!) '…they
deceive the minds of naïve people' (Romans 16:17–18). How are
we to be defended against false teachers who would trick us into
following them instead of following Christ? 'When the Advocate
comes,' Jesus told his followers at the end of his life, 'whom I will
send to you from the Father, the Spirit of truth who comes from
the Father, he will testify on my behalf' (John 15:26). It was that
Spirit of truth who transformed the disciples from their obtuse-
ness to their wisdom. It is the same Spirit who can give us the
ability to discern what is true and what is false and who can help
us to prepare for the coming of the king.

*Lord, I pray that you will help me to discern which leaders are teach-
ing your truth, to enable me to follow your straight path.*

RG

Don't panic

You will hear of wars and rumours of wars; see that you are
not alarmed, for this must take place, but the end is not yet...
Nation will rise against nation, and kingdom against kingdom,
and there will be famines and earthquakes in various places:
all this is but the beginning of the birth-pangs.

I expect many readers have experienced giving birth. Early
labour pains may be followed by birth two hours later, or two
days later, or the pains may even prove to be a false alarm and
nothing immediate follows. That is what it is like, Jesus tells us,
when we look for the 'signs of his coming'. 'Wars and rumours of
wars... nation against nation... famines and earthquakes...' It
sounds familiar: Kosovo, Northern Ireland, Israel, the Sudan;
human violence and natural disasters frequently dominate the
news and make it appear that wars and disasters are on the
increase. But remember Pompeii, the Crusades, the plague,
Napoleon, Amritsar—war and tragedy are not new phenomena.
Many have predicted the imminence of the end of the world,
and have even named a date for Jesus' return. Jesus said such
events would inevitably happen. We must not be alarmed.

What is our personal response to this? How are we to behave
during these times of 'labour pains'? We turn to the apostle John.
'Now, little children, abide in him, so that when he is revealed
we may have confidence and not be put to shame before him at
his coming' (1 John 2:28). When we are shocked at pictures of
the suffering we see almost daily on our TV screens, we grieve
for the sufferers, but our faith in God's sovereignty or his love
does not need to be shaken, even though we cannot understand
why he allows such tragedies. Job endured ghastly loss and pain,
and he was angry with God; he reckoned he did not deserve such
suffering. But eventually—in chapter 42—he could affirm his
trust in God who was truly in control.

Lord, help me to share Job's conviction in you, the God in control.

RG

Things won't be easy

They will hand you over to be tortured and will put you to death, and you will be hated by all nations because of my name. Then many will fall away... but the one who endures to the end will be saved.

I recently visited an Islamic country in the Middle East. There I met a Christian convert from Islam. He had spent a year in prison, suffering extensive torture, in the authorities' efforts to persuade him to renounce his faith and to betray others. How relevant for him these verses are! It is hardly surprising that some do turn away from their faith. We who live in a 'safer' climate should pray for Christians who suffer such aggressive persecution.

For most of us the negative influences are more subtle. But Jesus describes our situation, too. 'Because of the increase of lawlessness, the love of many will grow cold' (v. 12). We live in a secular climate where most people ignore God and—like a salty, seaside atmosphere which corrodes cars left standing outside—our Christian values are gradually eroded and our love for Christ easily fades. We rarely face outright persecution, but in a society where it is regarded as odd, no longer the 'done thing', to go to church, the Christian has to swim against the current of popular opinion. We need courage to insert into a conversation a comment that puts God's perspective on life or death, or to decline—graciously—an invitation that we know would detract from God's way for us. It is uncomfortable to be laughed at—or ignored—for your Christian faith. We all need to make sure our lights are shining as brightly as they were a year ago.

O Jesus, I have promised to serve thee to the end;
Be thou for ever near me, my master and my friend;
I shall not fear the battle if thou art by my side,
Nor wander from the pathway if thou wilt be my guide.
J.E. BODE (1816–74)

Read Matthew 24:9–13.

RG

Good news for the world

And this good news of the kingdom will be proclaimed throughout the world, as a testimony to all nations; then the end will come.

Last year I spent two weeks in Borneo, a country of big rivers and many waterways through the jungle. I heard of inland villages where the good news of Jesus has never reached, and of Christians who go on mission trips upriver to share the gospel with tribal people. 'This good news of the kingdom will be proclaimed throughout the world.' It is nearly two thousand years since Jesus died, and the gospel is still penetrating into corners of the world where his name has never been heard. There are other countries where militantly anti-Christian governments have forced Christians to go underground and believers risk their lives to worship, to read the Bible, even to share their faith with others.

This extension of the gospel of Christ's kingdom is one of the preludes to 'the end', to his return. How can we help this to happen when we are not all called to go to Borneo or Uzbekistan? Before his ascension Jesus promised to give us his Holy Spirit to enable us to be his witnesses. Maybe your next door neighbour is totally ignorant about Jesus—you may be the only Christian she knows. Pray for an opportunity to tell her about your faith in Jesus. Make time to find out as much as you can about the church in one particular country, so that you can give prayer and financial support intelligently.

For some, there will be a call from God to work overseas in the cause of the gospel. The nature of missionary work has changed in thirty years, but Christians willing to commit themselves to live and work overseas for the cause of the gospel are still needed. Living conditions will often not be easy, frustrations may abound; it may even be hard to see what difference you are making. But your reward will be in knowing that you are obeying Jesus.

Read Acts 1:6–8.

RG

A warning for the disciples

So when you see the desolating sacrilege standing in the holy place, as was spoken of by the prophet Daniel, then those in Judea must flee to the mountains... At that time there will be great suffering, such as has not been from the beginning of the world until now.

'When will this happen?' the disciples asked Jesus when he told them that 'not one stone will be left here upon another' of the magnificent, though unfinished, temple. Jesus does not answer the question directly; he does not tell them 'when' but he does tell them 'how'. Forty years after this conversation, in AD70, the Roman general Titus captured Jerusalem; the temple was demolished, and on the Mount of Olives, where they were was sitting, trees were replaced by crosses for crucifixion. So he tells them to flee from this horror. 'Don't delay. Don't go home to collect your belongings.' However, this is not to be when he returns, and he warns them again not to be deceived by the 'false messiahs and false prophets' that will appear.

At first sight this passage seemed irrelevant to me and I wondered what I could learn for my own life. Then these words struck me: 'The one on the housetop must not go down to take what is in the house; the one in the field must not turn back to get a coat' (vv. 17–18). That spoke to me about my need to sit loose to my possessions. I thought of the safety card in an aeroplane: 'If you have to evacuate, leave everything behind.' What! Even my passport and my handbag? How petty I am! Hurricane Mitch swept through Central America last year, leaving ten thousand people dead and millions without homes, possessions or means of livelihood. 'We brought nothing into the world, so that we can take nothing out of it,' Paul reminds us (1 Timothy 6:7). When Jesus returns, will he find us clutching our material goods? Or will he find us generous, not grasping?

Lord, I pray that your love may overcome my greed.
Read Matthew 24:15–25.

RG

A blaze of glory

*As the lightning comes from the east and flashes as far as the
west, so will be the coming of the Son of Man… They will see
'the Son of Man coming on the clouds of heaven' with power
and great glory. And he will send out his angels with a loud
trumpet call, and they will gather his elect from the four
winds, from one end of heaven to the other.*

Jesus' description of his return is dramatic. It will be no hole-in-
the-corner affair, but like lightning which flashes across the
whole sky. Read Paul's similar picture of Christ's coming, as he
writes to those who are worried about what will happen to
believers who have already died. 'The Lord himself, with a cry of
command, with the archangel's call and the sound of God's
trumpet, will descend from heaven, and the dead in Christ will
rise first. Then we who are alive, who are left, will be caught up
in the clouds together with them to meet the Lord in the air; and
so we will be with the Lord for ever' (1 Thessalonians 4:16–17).
Those early Christians thought that Jesus would come again in
their lifetime. Two millennia later we can be confident that all
who have been Christians down the centuries will together go to
be with him in eternity. And, whether we are alive or dead, we
can be equally confident that we will not miss this culminating
event of all history. May we live in such a way that we will not
need to be ashamed, however suddenly he comes.

Brothers, this Lord Jesus shall return again,
With his Father's glory, with his angel train;
For all wreaths of empire meet upon his brow
And our hearts confess him King of glory now.
C. NOEL (1817–77)

*So we pray with the hymn writer that we enthrone him in our hearts,
and 'let him subdue all that is not holy, all that is not true'.
Read Matthew 24:26–31.*

                                                              RG

No one knows

About that day and hour no one knows, neither the angels of heaven, nor the Son, but only the Father. For as the days of Noah were, so will be the coming of the Son of Man.

'When will it happen?' Most of us like to know what future events we can write in our diaries; it gives us a measure of security. But there is one question to which not even Jesus knew the answer: when will he come back? His return will be unmistakable and sudden. The people of Noah's time were corrupt and violent and God saw that 'the wickedness of humankind was great in the earth' (Genesis 6:5). People totally disregarded God and his ways; and the flood struck suddenly, without further time to change their lives. This is the abruptness, Jesus says, with which he will return. He will come without warning, like a burglar in the night.

So how can we be ready, if we too are to have no warning of his coming? John shows us how. 'When he is revealed, we will be like him, for we will see him as he is. And all who have this hope in him purify themselves, just as he is pure' (1 John 3:2–3). A life modelled on Jesus and his character; that is our response to the Father's immense love for us.

What will this mean in practice? It will mean love worked out in our relationships with family, friends, neighbours, colleagues. It will mean graciousness towards the surly, a smile towards a mother with a crying child, forgiveness towards those who wrong us, patience with roadhogs, an offer of help to the elderly, courtesy towards those who serve us, generosity to those who are worse off than we are. It will mean self-control in our personal habits and willingness to put ourselves out for other people's needs. Does that sound impossible? Not if we co-operate with the Spirit who wants his fruit to grow in our lives.

Lord, may I grow more like you and be ready for your return.
Read 1 Thessalonians 5:1–11.

RG

Keep awake! Be ready!

Keep awake therefore, for you do not know on what day your Lord is coming… Therefore you also must be ready, for the Son of Man is coming at an unexpected hour.

Jesus loved capturing people's attention with stories—and everyone loves a wedding! So he told a story about the bridesmaids at a wedding. Among their duties they were to meet the arriving bridegroom and escort him to the bride, lighting the way with their oil lamps. But on this occasion he was delayed, and they dozed off while they waited for him. Suddenly there was a shout: 'He's coming!' Five of them were prepared; they had spare oil and could refill their lamps. The rest had been careless; they woke with a start to found that their oil had run low. While they went to the store for a refill, the bridegroom came and the group went off. When the foolish ones arrived back, they were late; the door was shut. 'Lord, Lord, open to us!' was their cry. The reply was devastating: not just 'You're too late!' but 'I do not know you.'

We can prepare for a burglar with mortise locks and burglar alarms; but a burglar comes unannounced and takes us by surprise. Similarly, the bridesmaids had ample time to prepare for the bridegroom, but when he came, he came suddenly. So it is with Jesus' return. We need to be ready now, so when he comes he does not catch us off guard. How are we to be ready? Those words 'I do not know you' are the key. I heard of a three-year-old who has recently started to go to church. She told her grandmother, an ordained lady, 'I'm like you now. I know all about Jesus.' Granny: 'And do you know him?' Child, thoughtfully: 'Not yet.' There is a difference between knowing about a person and knowing them. If we are to be ready for Jesus' coming, we must know him as a friend, not just as a doctrine.

Read Matthew 25:1–13.

RG

Faithfulness rewarded

'Well done, good and trustworthy slave; you have been trust-worthy in a few things, I will put you in charge of many things; enter into the joy of your master.'

Another well-known story! This time Jesus uses the image of a businessman who goes away on a business trip and leaves his money in the care of three employeees: five talents (worth many thousands of pounds) for one, two for another, just one for the third. Although he does not give specific instructions, it is implied that they are to use the money for trading. The first two knew that their master would put this money to work, so by hard work, ingenuity and shrewdness, they doubled the money by the time their employer returned. 'Well done,' was his commendation. 'You have proved your reliability. I can trust you with more.'

What does this mean for us? The 'talents' do not represent either money or particular gifts and abilities (in the way we use the word 'talent'). Rather, they are the responsibilities God gives his people in the light of our abilities and circumstances. He wants to be able to rely on us to use faithfully and fruitfully the opportunities for service that he gives us. My own congregation has recently put out a leaflet for our annual 'Stewardship Sunday'. I like the acrostic on the cover: 'Christ gave everything. We give: Our time and talents, Understanding, Resources, Service, Energy, Love, Values, Earnings, Support.' OURSELVES. Each one of us is challenged to look at our lifestyle, our situation, our individual characteristics. It may seem obvious that God has given us many good things; others may appear to be impoverished in comparison. But he asks every one of us to be faithful in using for him whatever he has given us.

Thank you, Lord, for all the good things you give me. I pray that I may know how you want me to use them for you, and that I may fulfil your desires for me.

RG

Apparent injustice

Throw him into the outer darkness.

The story continues. The third man sees his master in a different way from the others. 'He's a hard man. I don't want to make a mistake and lose his money. I'll keep it really safe, and hide it where no one will steal it.' When his boss appeared he got it all out of its hiding-place; he put on a brave face as he said, 'Look, sir, here it is. I kept it safely for you. I was afraid I would lose it.' His master was furious. 'At least you could have got interest at the bank. Take him away; he's no good to me!'

This parable appears to deal with the contrast between the faithfulness and industry of some, and the idleness of others. There is reward for the hard-working and severe punishment for the lazy. But behind the behaviour is belief; behind the faithfulness there is faith. The men had different concepts of their master's character. Two saw him as one they could trust, for whom they wanted to work. The third one's perception was of a hard, greedy man of whom he was afraid. Much of our behaviour is determined by our perception of God's character. Do we see him as the hard, unfeeling, distant god who (like Islam's Allah) will be merciful if we're lucky? Or is he a God whose goodness, justice and love we can really trust? That is the God we will want to serve and to please.

God has shown us what he is like, both through the Bible (the written word) and through his Son, Jesus (the living Word). This man was thrown out because, at the basic level, he did not understand what his master was like. The foolish bridesmaids were excluded from the party because they were strangers to the bridegroom. Do you want to be included in Christ's 'party' when he comes again?

Lord, I pray that I may grow in understanding of your true character, and in knowing you as well as knowing about you.

RG

Separation—can it be true?

When the Son of Man comes in his glory, and all the angels with him, then he will sit on the throne of his glory. All the nations will be gathered before him, and he will separate people one from another as a shepherd separates the sheep from the goats, and he will put the sheep at his right hand and the goats at the left.

As a teenager I studied Matthew's Gospel for a public examination. I had no problem in believing Jesus' miracles, but there were many verses I wanted to cut out of his teaching. The clear separation of sheep from goats, wheat from weeds, good from bad fish; he used illustrations that were familiar to his largely rural audience to emphasize the finality of the judgment that awaits us—'Collect the weeds and bind them in bundles to be burned' (Matthew 13:30). I didn't like it. It did not fit with my concept of God's character. Surely a God of love would not act in such a harsh, destructive way? Many people are reluctant to believe that God will exclude anyone from his eternal kingdom.

Later I saw that a holy God who is a righteous judge cannot just overlook the misdemeanours of those who choose to ignore him. I had a glimpse of the utter, blinding purity of a God whose 'eyes are too pure to look on evil', who 'cannot tolerate wrong' (Habakkuk 1:13). If God were only holy like that we would all be eternally banished. But such holiness throws his love into sharp relief. Probably the best known verse in the Bible is John 3:16: 'God so loved the world that he gave his only Son, so that everyone who believes in him may not perish but may have eternal life.' His love is seen against a backdrop of the very real possibility that we might perish. Yes, there is eternal death as well as eternal life. The separation of 'sheep' from 'goats' is a reality.

When the Bible's teaching about God conflicts with my own ideas about him, which is most likely to be right?

RG

The king in disguise

The king will say to those at his right hand, 'Come, you that are blessed by my Father, inherit the kingdom prepared for you from the foundation of the world; for I was hungry and you gave me food, I was thirsty and you gave me something to drink, I was a stranger and you welcomed me.'

At first sight this passage seems to say that our acceptability to Christ is determined only by our good works in caring for the poor and needy—yet this contradicts much else that we read in the Bible. So what is Jesus telling us to expect when he comes in glory as king and as judge?

Jesus' first coming was in disguise, a baby born in a stable into a humble family. Throughout his life he identified with the poor, the downtrodden, the homeless: 'the Son of Man has nowhere to lay his head' (Luke 9:58). Much of his ministry was among the poor and the sick, among those who were outcast and despised. These people really mattered to him. And he expects the ways we show our love for him to include costly, practical care and love towards those who are so important to him, those with whom he identified.

Two beautiful stories are told. One is about Francis of Assisi, who came from a wealthy, upper-class family. One day, out riding, he met a hideous leper. He dismounted to hug him; as he did so the man's face was transformed into the face of Christ. We read, too, about Martin of Tours, a Roman soldier who was a Christian. One freezing day a beggar stopped him to ask for money. His pockets were empty, but he tore his cloak in two and gave one half to the beggar. That night in a dream he saw Jesus in heaven, wearing half his cloak, and heard an angel asking: 'Master, why are you wearing that old cloak?' Jesus replied, 'My servant Martin gave it to me.'

What will Jesus say to you when you meet him face to face?

RG

Judged—and found wanting

'Lord, when was it that we saw you hungry or thirsty or a
stranger or naked or sick or in prison, and did not take care of
you?' Then he will answer them, 'Truly I tell you, just as you
did not do it to one of the least of these, you did not do it to
me.' And these will go away into eternal punishment, but the
righteous into eternal life.

Each one of us is free to live our lives as we choose; but one day
God will call us to give account for our use of that freedom. Can
you imagine the line-up as we wait to face our maker? Jesus had
a solemn warning in the Sermon on the Mount: 'Not everyone
who says to me, "Lord, Lord," will enter the kingdom of heaven,
but only one who does the will of my Father in heaven. On that
day many will say to me, "Lord, Lord, did we not prophesy in
your name, and cast out demons in your name, and do many
deeds of power in your name?" Then I will declare to them, "I
never knew you; go away from me, you evildoers"' (Matthew
7:21–23). We might say, 'But Lord, I was in church every
Sunday... Lord, I ran the church bazaar for twenty years... Lord,
I read my Bible and said my prayers twice a day...' What if he
asks us: 'But where were you when the tramp came to the
door... When your neighbour was dying of cancer... When you
watched the television pictures of starving Sudanese...?' Would
we dare to tell him, 'Lord, I was too busy'?

    The chapter ends with some very unpalatable words, a
solemn warning of eternal punishment for those who have not
shown his love to others. These words are not to leave us frightened, but to spur us on to love Christ and to love people.

Ask Jesus for help to be aware of the needs around you today and to
respond to them.

RG

A message from Zechariah—
'Don't give up hope!'

Praise be to the Lord, the God of Israel, because he has come and has redeemed his people.

Tension on stage had reached an all-time high as harassed teachers pushed small actors into position for the infant school nativity play. Beyond the curtains, proud parents waited impatiently. As the curtains parted, Joseph was violently sick over Mary's blue costume. Enraged, she flung the plastic baby Jesus at a nearby shepherd and the back legs of the donkey tumbled off the stage, pulling the front legs after him. As irate teachers coped with the chaos, a troop of chubby angels tripped forward to chant, 'Christmas is all about peace and joy,' while a voice was heard to say, 'You could have fooled me!'

As a mother of six, I've been to my fair share of nativity plays but that was certainly the funniest! This year, as I watched my granddaughter's first performance, I thought, 'Wouldn't it be wonderful if the miniature actors melted away and the real characters were allowed to step down from heaven and talk to us.' Let's take an imaginary microphone and interview the elderly priest Zechariah first.

'Excuse me, Sir, now you've had plenty of time up there in heaven, have you a message for a group of women living two thousand years later in time?' Perhaps the old man would reply, 'Don't give up hope.' He waited a lifetime for a son. He and his wife prayed, probably fasted, wept and even bargained with God—and in the end they gave up hope. When an angel finally told Zechariah his prayers were answered, his faith had been so eroded by disappointment that he couldn't believe it was true.

Perhaps you prayed for years too for an unbelieving husband; a prodigal child; physical healing; marriage or a baby of your own? Perhaps, like Zechariah, you've given up bothering to ask.

Remember what the angel said to Mary? 'Nothing is impossible with God' (Luke 1:37).

JRL

A message from the shepherds—
'Take time to be still'

*Be still, and know that I am God; I will be exalted among the
nations, I will be exalted in the earth!*

'Christmas has become so commercialized and pressured these
days.' How often we hear that! Yet the first Christmas Eve in
Bethlehem was just the same as 'late-night Christmas shopping'
in any town nowadays. The streets surged with visitors, business
boomed for market traders and innkeepers, parties and family
reunions took place all over town and everyone was too busy
cooking, eating, laughing, quarrelling and making love to look up
at the sky. Perhaps the shepherds, sitting on the hillside, saw the
lights of the town in the distance and wished they could join the
fun, but if they had not stayed still under the stars they would
have missed the biggest angelic display ever performed outside
heaven! If we were to interview those shepherds now, they might
say, 'Take time to sit still.'

'Fat chance, this time of year!' most women would reply
indignantly. 'They should just see my jobs list!' Yet we, like the
busy inhabitants of Bethlehem, can become so 'earthbound' that
we forget the supernatural world—the eternal dimension—
which surrounds us. Jesus had two friends—sisters, one called
Martha, who was always cooking, doing, dashing, and Mary, who
just wanted to sit next to him, as close as she could get. Martha
tried to please Jesus by her activity, but it was company he longed
for most. The Martha side of us can get so busy this time of year
that the Mary in us disappears under piles of washing-up. The gift
of our time is the most precious Christmas present we can offer to
God, and he understands if we can only give him as long as it
takes to boil the kettle!

*Lord, you know how busy I am at present, but please help me to find
little odd moments to be with you during the next two weeks. Let my
spirit dance and sing with the angels as I look up at the sky, beyond
all the entertaining, TV and last-minute shopping. Amen*

JRL

A message from the innkeeper's wife— 'Open your door'

'When did we see you a stranger and invite you in?' ... The King will reply, 'I tell you the truth, whatever you did for one of the least of these brothers of mine, you did for me.'

The Bible doesn't mention an innkeeper's wife—but someone must have offered Joseph and Mary their stable.

We too can get so absorbed in giving our families a fabulous Christmas that we forget many people are 'left out in the cold' to spend the holiday alone. Christmas can make loneliness, singleness, chronic illness and old age feel a hundred times worse. So an invitation to share a family meal can mean the world. My heart sinks as I write that. The people I feel I 'ought' to ask are usually the ones who are 'difficult' and ruin the party! But I guess Mary in labour didn't look a very attractive guest either.

I once watched a TV programme about Mother Teresa. She was washing the body of a dying man. He was filthy and covered with ulcers, yet she cared for him with astounding gentleness and respect. 'To me he is Jesus,' she said, 'What an honour to ease my Lord's pain.'

Brother Tom, a monk, was the cook in a local monastery. One day he told me about a dream he'd had.

'Jesus himself came to the door, saying he was hungry. I rushed to cook him the best meal ever and finally placed before him fish, covered in creamy sauce, fluffy mashed potatoes, and buttery peas—but I woke before I saw him enjoying it. Next day, a tramp arrived just after I had taken dinner into the refectory. All I had left was my own plate of food. Grudgingly I handed it to him, then realized it was fish covered in sauce with potatoes, and peas! I was so moved I had a job hiding my tears.'

Lord, I invite you to come to my home this Christmas, in any disguise you choose.

JRL

A message from the angels—
'Enjoy yourselves!'

Suddenly a great company of the heavenly host appeared with the angel, praising God and saying, 'Glory to God in the highest, and on earth peace to men on whom his favour rests.'

The Bible tells us that angels think, talk, learn and have feelings. They are very powerful and can move rapidly about the universe. Above all they totally trust God and exist to serve and worship him. How frustrated they must get when they see our doubts, disobedience and lack of love!

When they finally realized that God was planning to step down to earth, to show us the extent of his love, they must have been delighted. They must have been amazed when he became smaller than a pin-head and tucked himself away inside the uterus of a mere woman. And I wonder what they thought when they realized that the hands which had rolled the planets off into space had become pink baby fists; the eyes that looked out across the galaxies were tight shut in the liquid darkness of the womb and the heart that beat with compassion for the entire universe lay in the fluttering rib cage of a foetus.

When they finally heard the voice which had spoken the universe into existence sounding like a squeaky birth cry, they simply could not contain themselves. They burst out of heaven, filling the skies with light, music and triumphant dance.

Perhaps the angels get fed up with us each year when we grumble about expense, boring telly and lack of help with the washing-up! I think they long for us to enjoy the celebration—just as they did.

Oh Lord, I do want to enjoy Christmas and to stop all these negative thoughts but it would be far easier to worship if I were flying around up there in the sky, free of all these demanding people. Help me, even stuck down here in the mess of my kitchen, to worship you with all my heart. Amen

JRL

A message from Joseph—
'Don't risk it!'

Because Joseph her husband was a righteous man and did not want to expose her to public disgrace, he had in mind to divorce her quietly.

Joseph has become a mere Christmas card character, but he was a real man with deep feelings. Just before his wedding, the bride he loved suddenly went off to the sophisticated south country for three months. When she came home she was pregnant. 'But it's all right,' she said. 'An angel told me the baby is God's son.'

Every girl who ever got into trouble invented some sort of story. Joseph must have felt hurt, betrayed and downright angry. We don't know how long he struggled with his pain; it might have been weeks. He had every right to demand that Mary was stoned to death by the men of the village—and, legally, he could throw the first stone.

When the person you love best humiliates, betrays and lies to you, stoning can seem like a soft punishment; but gradually Joseph reached the decision to let Mary off what he thought she deserved. He didn't believe her, but he wanted to forgive. It was not until he had reached that decision that the angel was able to come and reassure him that Mary could be trusted. A blessing always follows the decision to forgive.

What if, like so many of us, Joseph had resolutely refused to forgive—held on to his hurt and allowed justice to take its course. Perhaps God would have found another way to protect Mary, but what a lot Joseph would have missed!

Has someone hurt you badly—dumped you, destroyed your life? The anger and pain we feel as a result of their actions are like chains that keep us trapped in a lonely prison. Why not decide now, before Christmas and a new millennium, to let that anger go—spit out the hate and breathe in the love of Jesus. Freedom and a new life follow that decision. Not forgiving simply doesn't seem worth the risk.

JRL

A message from Mary—
'Acceptance brings peace'

Then Mary said, 'Here am I, the servant of the Lord; let it be with me according to your word.'

Suppose Mary hadn't answered Gabriel like that? Instead she might have said a firm 'No way! I don't want to risk losing the man I love, or being stoned to death. I'd hate to be an outcast and a refugee and I don't want to watch my son tortured to death in front of my eyes.'

God would have found someone else, but Mary would not have been used by God and called 'blessed' by every generation since.

'God, this just isn't fair!' we feel like shouting when he asks us to care for a disabled relative day in, day out, with no help or recognition from others; to grind on through a loveless marriage or to stay sick while others are healed.

It's hard to face the fact that God doesn't always make life cosy for us, any more than he did for Mary. He sometimes asks us to serve him in the most unattractive ways with no audience to cheer us on or even notice our efforts. But arguing with him, demanding a better deal or trying to manipulate him into doing what we want, only robs us of our peace.

David once prayed, 'Restore to me the joy of your salvation and grant me a willing spirit, to sustain me' (Psalm 51:12). I am sure the two things go together—the joy and the willingness. And it is the willingness which gives us the strength to carry on. If God asked you to found the most successful church in the world, be a female Billy Graham or heal every sick person you met, wouldn't you accept eagerly? Perhaps he's asking us to do something far harder than that—to be his faithful servant, cheerfully doing exactly what we have to do today.

'Father, if you are willing, take this cup from me; yet not my will, but yours be done' (Luke 22:42).

JRL

A message from the baby Jesus— 'I am the best present you'll ever have!'

For God so loved the world that he gave his one and only Son, that whoever believes in him shall not perish but have eternal life.

Such a tiny bundle, weighing less than most Christmas turkeys. Yet he came to bring us so much! Life that will never end, not just in heaven; he said he had also come to bring us abundant life down here on earth (John 10:10). He wants us to live to the full in this new millennium. That sounds impossible for many of us whose lives are extremely tough. Yet even when things are at their worst, he gives us his own brand of peace and joy—that inexplicable sense of inner well-being which has nothing whatsoever to do with the outer events of our lives.

Most of all, he came to be *there* for us—not just at special times like Christmas, but always. *There* for us when we wake alone and afraid in the night. *There* for us when we just don't know what to do for the best. *There* for us, sharing our happiness. *There* with us to give us his strength when all our own has oozed away. *There* with us to give us courage to walk up to our worst fear when we want to run away. *There* for us when we've 'messed up' yet again—said or done the very thing we wanted to avoid! *There* for us when someone cuts us to pieces and doesn't even realize what they've done. *There* for us when absolutely no one else is.

What a Christmas present! Who needs anything else?

But I have a friend who, because of an awful childhood experience, can never bring himself to open Christmas presents. He carefully puts them on one side and just looks at them. I guess lots of us treat Jesus like that. A present has to be unwrapped, used and enjoyed.

O come to my heart, Lord Jesus, there is room in my heart for thee.
EMILY ELLIOTT (1836–97)

JRL

Matthew 2:1–12 (NIV)

A message from the wise men—'Go for it!'

When they saw the star, they were overjoyed. On coming to the house, they saw the child with his mother Mary, and they bowed down and worshipped him. Then they opened their treasures and presented him with gifts of gold and of incense and of myrrh.

Most children long to play one of the three grandly dressed kings in the nativity play, but the Bible never says there were three, or that they were kings. And they certainly didn't arrive at Christmas—it had to be at least six weeks later. So who were they?

They were astrologers and they also knew the scriptures intimately. They honoured and obeyed God and believed in angels. But the thing I like best about them is their enthusiasm! When they saw the star they set off at once on the dangerous, costly journey to worship the Messiah.

They also might have thought, 'There's too much on to go right now; this trip could easily wait until next year.' But God needed their gifts to finance the trip to Egypt. Joseph and Mary were too poor to afford a long journey with hotel bills, feed for the donkey and a new home to find and equip. If the gold and expensive spices had not arrived at exactly the right moment, the little family might not have escaped so completely from Herod's evil clutches. God needed those wise men to be at the right place, at the right time, with the right gifts.

As you look ahead into a new millennium, do you sense God is calling *you* to do something new for him? A job, a role at church, voluntary work? Perhaps you've been thinking about it for ages but somehow…? I believe the wise men would say to all of us, 'Get up and go for it! God needs people like you to serve him in his new millennium.'

OK, Lord, I'll go for it, but only if you hold my hand!

JRL

A message from the donkey— 'Carry him with you'

An angel… appeared to Joseph in a dream. 'Get up,' he said, 'take the child and his mother and escape to Egypt.'

I heard a story recently about the young donkey who carried Jesus into Jerusalem on the first Palm Sunday. When he arrived home that evening he said, 'Mum, I'm famous! Everyone cheered me, waved palms and made me a "red carpet" from coats!'

'Silly boy!' snorted his mother. 'It wasn't *you* they were cheering, it was your rider!'

Of course we don't *know* there was a donkey in the Christmas story, but Mary could hardly run all the way to Egypt with a tiny baby in her arms. Perhaps the donkey didn't like being woken in the night and ridden at speed down a strange road which definitely did not lead to his own familiar stable. What if he so hated the thought of Egypt that he behaved like many donkeys do and just stopped dead, refusing to budge? Herod's soldiers would have been there before Joseph could have found the nearest carrot!

Horror stories have been circulating for months about all that might go wrong in the new millennium. What if our civilization really is crashed by our computers? Or high-tech war demolishes us all? What if the food chain becomes seriously contaminated or world dictatorship takes over? All that is very frightening for many of us but we don't have to enter this period of history alone. If we are Christians, we take Jesus with us as a donkey carries its rider. So long as we allow him to take the 'reigns' of our lives and choose the route, instead of digging in our hooves stubbornly, we will be safe. Allow him to take you into every situation you face in this new millennium.

So do not fear, for I am with you; do not be dismayed, for I am your God. I will strengthen you and help you; I will uphold you with my righteous right hand. (Isaiah 41:10)

JRL

No message from Herod

If we confess our sins, he is faithful and just and will forgive us our sins and purify us from all unrighteousness.

Somehow I just can't picture Herod sending us a message from heaven. Surely there is no crime more deserving of hell than killing innocent babies. Yet the incredible thing is that the very baby he was trying to destroy was his only hope for eternity.

The main reason Jesus came to earth was to die a cruel death so that he could take the rap for men like Herod. If he repented and asked for God's forgiveness during the last two years of his life, he will be there in heaven waiting for us. So might Hitler and all child molesters, torturers and killers—if they repented. Such is the forgiving grace of Jesus.

This past millennium, the sheer weight of human misery caused by evil people towards the innocent is staggering. We seem to be growing more horrible to one another. Yet, by dying on the cross, Jesus made it possible for us all to be forgiven. We only have to ask.

As the last few grains of sand trickle through the hour-glass of this present millennium, we can't do much about all those millions of Herods who have caused others to suffer; we are not responsible for their sin. But we are responsible for our own.

I'm going to carve out some space before next Friday night to ask the Holy Spirit to give me a thorough clean-out. I want him to show me all the things I do which upset him and cause problems for others. All the sins I've stuffed away at the back of my memory and never owned up to, all the little habits or thought patterns which are impeding my spirit and stunting its growth. I long to walk into this new millennium clean, with my head held high, not because of my good behaviour but because of what Jesus did for me on the cross.

JRL

A message from Simeon—
'Don't ignore the nudge!'

There was a man in Jerusalem called Simeon… Moved by the Spirit, he went into the temple courts. When the parents brought in the child Jesus…

Suppose you were snoozing in the sun when you 'felt' the Lord tell you to hurry off to church and meet a visiting baby? Most of us would tell ourselves firmly that we were imagining things and forget about the inner 'nudge'. But Simeon didn't. He had waited a lifetime to see the Messiah, so when he felt the Lord say, 'Go to the temple,' he went and was there in time to hold the baby in his arms.

I believe God uses all kinds of ways to speak to us: the Bible, sermons, other Christians, nature, circumstances. But I also believe he sometimes communicates directly, just as he did with Simeon. One Saturday, Janet left the kids with her mother and went Christmas shopping—on her own! She was having a lovely leisurely browse when she felt God telling her to visit a friend called Anne. Janet's heart sank. Anne had been depressed since her marriage broke up, and Janet didn't really want to visit her. But the nudge continued, until Janet reluctantly gave up her planned tea and walked down to Anne's house. No one answered the door for a long time, and when Janet looked through the letter box she saw Anne's body slumped on the sofa. When the police and ambulance men finally got in, they discovered she had taken a massive overdose but they had arrived just in time. If Janet had not arrived when she did, it would have been all over.

I've heard too many stories like that to ignore a nudge. God is moving so rapidly these days, he needs our attention, instantly. If things get sticky in the new millennium, he is going to have to move us round more rapidly than ever before. Listening for and responding to the 'nudge' is a skill that requires constant practice.

Lord, please give me acute inner hearing and the courage to act on what I hear. Amen

JRL

A message from Anna—
'God's servants never retire!'

She never left the temple but worshipped night and day, fasting and praying.

Recently, a departing guest presented me with a gorgeous bunch of flowers—which gave me enormous pleasure for two weeks. Returning from a weekend away, I realized they'd 'had it' at last—except for one lily which I saved in a vase on my desk. Miraculously it retained its creamy perfection for ten more days. When a group of friends came to pray we spent ten silent minutes 'considering the lily of the field' then shared the various ways it had spoken into our lives.

Most women over forty hate the thought of old age, which robs us of our looks, figure and status in the world. Anna was probably over one hundred, yet that day in the temple she was 'centre stage'. After seven years of marriage, tragedy hit her life—but had not blighted it. She handled her grief by living constantly in God's presence—talking to him about the people she met and talking to the people she met about him.

All of us will grow old in this new millennium. Many, like Anna, will face bereavement, loneliness or poverty but, like my lily, will we go on giving pleasure to our 'owner' and being used by him to bless others? Anna's secret was that she remained in the temple, but we don't have to camp out at church! We can remain in his presence simply by realizing that he is always right beside us.

Lord, help me to cultivate the habit of chatting to you constantly— telling you what I'm doing, sharing jokes, inwardly praying for people around me and thanking you for every beautiful thing I see. You once said, 'Planted in the house of the Lord, they will flourish in the courts of our God. They will still bear fruit in old age, they will stay fresh and green, proclaiming, "The Lord is upright"' (Psalm 92:13–15). Lord, that's what I want to do, right to the end of my life. Amen

JRL

A message from the whole cast—'Make it count!'

Therefore, since we are surrounded by such a great cloud of witnesses, let us throw off everything that hinders and the sin that so easily entangles, and let us run with perseverance the race marked out for us.

We've reached the finale of our grand nativity play and I think all the human members of the cast would be eager to say just one last thing to us before the curtain falls.

After enjoying two thousand years of heaven, can they even remember those brief years on planet Earth? How do their difficulties and disappointments appear when viewed from eternity?

Our 'main characters' realize now that what we do here is vital and actually makes a difference when we arrive in heaven. Life gives us our chance to do the greatest possible thing for our families, friends and neighbours—show them the way to live happily for ever. It's also our chance to get to know the king of heaven as an intimate friend, so that he isn't only a distant figure, seen and admired by us from a vast distance. It is also our chance to turn our pain and sadness into the eternal 'treasures of darkness' (Isaiah 45:3). We cannot earn our ticket to heaven, but when we arrive, the size of our reward depends on our faithfulness down here (Luke 19:12–26).

Whatever we all have to face during this new millennium, when we have been 'up there' two thousand years our troubles will appear 'light and momentary… achieving for us an eternal glory that far outweighs them all' (2 Corinthians 4:17).

So, before this millennium finally dies, let's make a new commitment to give ourselves to the Lord one hundred per cent as we step into a new phase of history—whatever it may hold.

But one thing I do: forgetting what is behind and straining towards what is ahead, I press on towards the goal to win the prize for which God has called me heavenwards in Christ Jesus. (Philippians 3: 13–14)

JRL

DAY BY DAY WITH GOD

MAGAZINE SECTION

The millennium —and all that...

Mary Reid

So here we are—about to begin the third millennium. To be more accurate, we are about to begin the year 2000—it becomes the third millennium at the beginning of 2001! My mind has become boggled with all the talk and excitement and *fuss* surrounding what is nothing more than the clock moving on from midnight and into another day.

Computer experts have been working overtime for months to ensure that our sophisticated world systems don't crash because we have run out of 1900s! There has been talk of making sure we have a good supply of tinned and frozen foods stocked in our cupboards 'just in case' there is millennium chaos in the food market—and the money market—and everything else that now relies on computer control. Does this mean that I may not get billed for gas, electricity and water?

Lost memory
What I do know—and not everyone getting excited about the millennium celebration realizes—is that it marks two thousand years since God sent his Son as a baby into our world so that everyone who believes in him may not die, but have eternal life (John 3:16, GNB). We live in a society that seems to have lost its memory of this fact.

When I started out as a Christian the world seemed much bigger. Space had not been explored—even travelling overseas was a great adventure. Now my daughter hops on a plane for a meeting on the Continent and is home in time for tea (well, almost). We watch wars actually happening from the comfort of our centrally heated homes. We accept, without surprise, that the space shuttle will take people regularly up to a space station to replenish supplies for those already there, or to add yet another section to the platform. All this change in just fifty years. So what about the next fifty years? What will life be like for today's children when they are the older generation? When we try to look ahead, do we feel there is something to celebrate?

Another thing has changed for me too. When I was a new Christian I used to almost envy the thief crucified alongside Christ. Jesus said to him, 'I promise you that today you will be in Paradise with me' (Luke 23:43, GNB). How wonderful to know that Paradise was so near. Now I am older I don't feel the same impatience—maybe because there is so much in this life that I want to hang on to. I enjoy being alive and having a family to love. I love walking in the countryside in all weathers. Life at the moment is good, and I would like to feel it will stay that way for quite a long time yet. There is so much to *do* that is worth while and not enough time to look too far ahead. But the millennium is making us stop and look the future in the face—and this has to be a good thing.

This is God's world—and, as I heard someone once say, he wants it back! In spite of the doom and gloom that batters us from the media there are good things happening, and we are each a vital part of God's plan in the year 2000.

Future hope

As Christians we do have a hope for the future—both while we are here on earth and when we join our Father in that eternal place that we can only wonder about, where 'there will be no more death, no more grief or crying or pain' (Revelation 21:4, GNB) and where 'calves and lion cubs will feed together, and little children will take care of them' (Isaiah 11:6, GNB). We have a lot to look forward to, both in the here-and-now world where the clock ticks relentlessly on—and in a glorious future when time doesn't matter and a thousand years is just like a day.

Our hope is in Christ—what about those who don't yet have this hope? What do they look forward to in the year 2000? What will they be celebrating on the eve of the new millennium? In a society that has developed a very materialistic set of values it seems that it is all going to be a huge New Year's Eve party. For this reason the Churches Together in England have prepared the Millennium Resolution to encourage everyone (those with faith and those with no faith) to join together in a shared moment of national reflection on New Year's Eve 1999:

Let there be
respect for the earth,
peace for its people,
love in our lives,
delight in the good,
forgiveness for past wrongs
and from now on a new start.

Every statement in this resolution comes from key Bible passages (*see below*) and if everyone who joins in making this a resolution (not only Christians) actually follows up the words with action and changed attitudes, then AD2000 has to be better than 1999!

A new start

It gives us all the chance to make a new start. As Christians we are constantly reassured through scripture that what we do in life is part of God's plan—and that nothing is ever a 'waste of time' when we commit it to God. Jesus gave us the words that we now call The Lord's Prayer—a perfect prayer for us as we try to make a new start. 'Hallowed be your name': we treat as holy the name of God; 'Your kingdom come': we want to live our lives knowing that God's kingdom has begun and that we are part of it; 'Your will be done on earth, as it is in heaven': we will try to live in accordance with the teaching of Jesus, no matter how small and insignificant that may seem to us. What an aim for the future—the coming of the year 2000 is going to be worth celebrating.

Some of the key biblical passages which underlie the Millennium Resolution:

Respect for the earth—Genesis 1:1; Romans 8:19-21

Peace for its people—John 14:27; 2 Thessalonians 3:16

Love in our lives—Matthew 22:37, 39; Romans 12:10

Delight in the good—Genesis 1:31; Matthew 5:16

Forgiveness for past wrongs—Luke 6:37; 11:4

And from now on a new start—2 Corinthians 5:17; Lamentations 3:22–23; Revelation 21:5

When God seems far away

Molly Dow

All relationships have their ups and downs, including very close, loving and intimate ones. When close, warm relationships lose their sparkle and become dull and dry, it can seem rather alarming. Has love fizzled out? When, if ever, will the sparkle return? This may sound like a lead in to something on marriage, but in fact I am thinking of our relationship with God (which does have some parallels with marriage and close friendships). What happens when our relationship with God loses its sense of life and sparkle?

When we lose the awareness of God's presence and loving care for us, we say we are spiritually dry or experiencing 'desert' times. They may creep up on us gradually, or descend suddenly, like a blanket of grey cloud. Either way, it is a hard experience, as God seems so distant.

The prayers we send out don't seem to arrive anywhere—at least, we don't hear any answer coming back. Our praying feels like speaking into thin air. As well as feeling frustrated, we may feel alone and abandoned by God. We may also feel ashamed and embarrassed: 'Surely this isn't meant to happen... I bet no one else has these problems... I must be a real failure as a Christian.'

Sometimes it is only a small step from saying that God *feels* far away to saying that he is actually absent. We may even doubt if he exists at all, and the sense of desolation can be very painful. Experience tells us, however, that these times are normal (most of us meet them more than once) and don't last for ever, that they can have positive value and that there are ways of helping ourselves through them.

It is encouraging to know that others have had such experiences too. Psalm 22 begins, 'My God, my God, why have you forsaken me? Why are you so far from helping me, from the words of my groaning? O my God, I cry by day, but you do not answer; and by night, but find no rest' (NRSV). The psalmist knew what desolation feels like. And Jesus used these words on the cross. Surely he understands too.

You do not answer

One of my toughest desert experiences was in my second year at university and included doubting almost everything about the Christian faith. I asked, 'Does God exist? Does he care about me? Is he the loving person Christians say he is? Are the Gospels reliable accounts of Jesus' life and teaching? Did Jesus really rise from the dead?' and so on and so on. I felt very alone. It was awful to think that there might be no God. I had been a Christian since my early teens and my relationship with God was very important to me. If he did not exist, what had been going on at those times when I thought I was experiencing him? And yet I was afraid of persuading myself into faith just because I *wanted* to believe. I wanted to know the truth, whether it turned out to be God or not, and to follow it, but how could I ever be sure of where the truth lay?

I have been through several times of feeling like this and have read about others' experiences too. Of course, each time for each person is unique, but there are some general lessons to be drawn.

Why do we go through these times?

Many factors can contribute to our desert times. Some may be physical, such as being ill, tired or run down. Some are emotional, such as stress, loss or bereavement. Others are spiritual.

Sin separates people from God (Isaiah 59:1–2). Sometimes it is our own sin that causes the dryness—but this is usually only when sin is wilful and persistent. Some people jump to this conclusion too quickly and need to beware of false or excessive guilt. Others may be slow to face up to their own responsibility. We do well to know ourselves over this, and to have others who can help us.

Sometimes it seems to be simply that God decides to remove from us the sense of his presence for the sake of our spiritual growth. Like a mother weaning her child, God may lead us to let go of old ways in order to move us on to greater maturity. He may, for example, use it to show us more about ourselves and our weakness, or more of himself and his grace. Desert times also show us that we cannot force God to give us a sense of his presence and peace by 'pressing the right spiritual buttons', such as prayer, or going to church. And the desert can be a challenge and an opportunity to show that we love God for his own sake, not just for what we get out of him.

When I was going through my desert time as a student, one of the most helpful things was when a friend pointed me to Deuteronomy 8:2, which speaks of God using the Israelites' forty years in the wilderness to show whether they really wanted to follow him. It says, 'God has led you... in the wilderness... to know what was in your heart' (NRSV). Like the Israelites, the very bleakness I was feeling gave me a chance to show God that I loved him for his sake, not only for my own benefit. Following God can feel very worthwhile when our lives are going smoothly and our faith brings us peace, joy, friends, comfort and other good things. We have feelings of love for God and want to serve him because of what we receive. But following him when things are difficult or boring, requiring mostly effort and struggle, is rather different. Yet it gives us an opportunity to choose to give him a love that has a minimum of self-interest about it. Love in the Bible is more about what we choose than how we feel.

Desert times may actually strengthen us as our faith and other gifts and qualities are stretched to the limit. Just as our muscles are strengthened by exercise, so can our faith be strengthened by having to use it, as we try to walk with God and keep close to him in the desert.

Survival tactics

I have found these helpful. You may like to try some, or all, of them.

Check for 'natural causes'

Sometimes the reason for a spiritually dry time lies in our circumstances. If we are unwell or tired, the whole of our life is affected, including our relationship with God. The same applies when we are bereaved, or suffering from other kinds of loss and stress. Then we need to be kind to ourselves.

Ask God to show you if your own sin has been a contributory cause

It is always true that our behaviour and attitudes have been less than perfect, but the question is whether or not God is allowing the desert experience in order to put his finger on something particular. Our sin may not be a cause at all, but the possibility can usefully be checked out, perhaps with a wise pastor, to help us guard against false guilt.

Keep in touch with God

This means being open and honest with him about what we are thinking, feeling and wanting. God wants to relate to the person we really are, not the person we may pretend to be. Sometimes it is the desert that forces us to face who and what we really are, as it strips us of our props and 'comfort blankets'. Although this can make us feel scared and vulnerable, it has the enormous benefit that it clears the way for us to meet God more truly and deeply. It enables us to move forward with him in a freer way.

Our prayers are likely to be short and to the point, like 'God, if you're there, help!' or 'Why don't you do something?' 'Lord, help me to trust you', 'Help me to keep going' and 'I've had enough!'

We may like to pray familiar prayers we know by heart, such as the Lord's Prayer and the Jesus Prayer ('Lord Jesus Christ, have mercy on me'). Some psalms and hymns that capture our mood can be helpful when we are stuck for our own words. They remind us that others have felt dry and desolate too, which can be comforting.

It is not easy to know whether to try to keep to our normal prayer routine, because of its helpful familiarity, or to try new patterns of prayer. Sometimes God uses the desert experience to move us out of old ways of praying into new ways that are now better for our spiritual growth and well-being. Here, too, a wise and experienced Christian friend or pastor can be most valuable.

Concentrate on praise and thanksgiving
However little we may feel like doing this, it will build faith, reminding us of God's goodness and his gifts to us. It is good to be as specific as possible. We may find a hymn or psalm of praise, such as Psalm 103, helpful.

We can also thank God for whatever good he will bring out of the time of difficulty. This doesn't mean pretending that the difficulty itself is good when it isn't.

Keep in touch with the church
Another helpful thing that was said to me in my desert time as a student was that I should not cut myself off from Christian worship and fellowship, since that was one of God's most likely ways of getting through to me again. I followed this advice, although it was very hard to sit through services and meetings where people were saying, praying and singing things I couldn't enter into. I am not aware that it helped me back to faith, but it did mean that when my faith was rekindled I didn't have to make a self-conscious return to the Christian community.

Look upwards and outwards
Although it may seem at times that our desert is all there is, this is obviously not true. Making the effort to concentrate more on God and on other people will help us to see things in better perspective. It is also part of seeking to love God and our neighbour for his or her sake, rather than ours.

Turn to your basic rations
Go to familiar verses and passages of scripture that you know and love. Read them, and let them comfort and strengthen you. You do not have to work at them, merely allow them to be there alongside you as friends. I once heard Cardinal Basil Hume say, 'Make friends among the psalms'. There are psalms to meet many different moods, and it is good to be able to find our own favourites when we need them. Favourite hymns, poetry and books can be sustaining too, especially when they

show us that someone else has felt similarly. They help us to feel understood and, therefore, less isolated.

Consider seeking some pastoral help
A wise, mature Christian who is not embroiled in the situation can help us to discern what God is saying and doing with us.

If you can, ask one or two trusted friends to pray for you (and with you). When we find it hard to pray for ourselves, it is very supportive to have others pray for us.

Hang on in there
Remind yourself that such experiences are quite common and they do come to an end. Try to be patient and to trust God to bring you through. Having been through several such times now, I find this easier to believe than I did the first time. I expect others would say the same. Why not ask them?

Molly Dow has a degree in chemistry and a diploma in theology, and is a Church of England Reader and Diocesan Spirituality Adviser. She is the author of *Mountains and Molehills* (Triangle, 1997), and is married to the Bishop of Willesden.

Looking to the future

Alie Stibbe

Alie Stibbe writes about the challenges of facing a new chapter in life.

I remember lying in bed when I was eight years old and thinking that I would be forty years old in the year 2000. Then it seemed a long way away. However, I now find myself with the new millennium tapping on my shoulder! Not only will I be forty, but my youngest child will start school that year. I will be left standing on the threshold of a major new chapter of my life just at the same time as we stand on the threshold of a major new chapter in history. It is quite a daunting thought. It will be a time for reassessment, new challenges and big decisions.

No change

At the turn of the year in the past, I have listened to Big Ben strike twelve and nothing has changed when it has finished. I am still standing in the same place with the same problems, the same hang-ups and the same people! I am the same person and the only thing that has changed, besides the position of the hands on the clock, is that I may have resolved, with God's help, to try and change something of myself or my immediate environment for the better. I think that it could be the same when the clock strikes on 31 December 1999. We will all stand there expecting something to change in the twinkling of an eye and we will all be dumbfounded to discover everything is the same as it was a few moments before!

The only thing we can be certain about in the run-up to the new millennium is that when the hour turns, we will be the same people, whatever the outward circumstances around us become, and that none of us will know any better then what the future will hold (Ecclesiastes 8:7). Only God knows what the future holds and it is our job to trust that he will guide us through what unfolds as it presents itself, whether for the better or the worse (Proverbs 3:5–6). 'For I know the plans I have for you,' declares the Lord, 'plans to prosper you and not to harm you, plans to give you hope and a future' (Jeremiah 29:11). If we can trust that the Lord has a hopeful future planned for us, the thing that we can do in response to that is to prepare ourselves for it in the present.

God's perfect plan

When we trust that God has a perfect plan for our lives, we know that everything that happens to us is for a purpose, whether for that particular instant, or as an investment for the future. What we have to do is allow ourselves to be open to the transforming work of the Holy Spirit in our hearts moment by moment, day by day so that our on-going attitude to God, even in the bleak moments, is an unequivocal, 'Yes, Lord!' This is a valuable spiritual attribute to be cultivated, and involves practising listening, even to what we don't want to hear, and obedience, even when we are full of self-pity and stubbornness. If we are committed to this, we are committed to change and be changed, for the better in whatever circumstances we may find ourselves (2 Corinthians 3:18).

The mistake that we often make is to assume that the preparation time is going to be easy! Often it isn't. More often than not, it is through the fire of suffering that we are changed into what the Lord wants us to be in order to be ready for the thing he has planned for us (James 1:2–4, 12; 1 Peter 1:6–7). In those times, God can often feel very absent from us and it is only by faith and an act of the will that we can continue to persevere.

When I think about this, I remember the story of Esther in the Old Testament. What happened to her was utterly demeaning. Her parents died young, perhaps tragically. She was brought up by an uncle, who possibly had designs to marry her when she came of age. Then she was forced, on pain of death, into the harem of a pagan king. One can hardly dare imagine what she perhaps had to force herself to do to become his favourite and then his queen. Where was God in all this? Some might say it would have been more heroic to have owned up to her nationality and beliefs and died for them to start with! Then it just 'happens' that she is found to be in the right place at the right time and given the strength and commitment to perform an act of daring and cunning that saves God's people in that whole empire. As her uncle says, 'And who knows but that you have come to this royal position [through all the suffering you have had to experience—implied] for such a time as this!' (Esther 4:14b, NIV). God was there, orchestrating events in the background, although at the time no one could have perceived it.

Nothing is wasted

I struggle terribly with being tied to the home by young children, often to the extent of feeling like a bird that is tethered by the foot. There are some very dark times for me, especially when I get over-tired. However, I constantly try to remind myself that nothing we go through is wasted for those that love the Lord and are trying to do his will (however hard they find it and however odd the struggle may seem to those on the outside) (Romans 8:28). In our everyday experience we have to believe that the Lord has a sovereign purpose for us.

In all this I am not trying to advocate that in difficult circumstances we sit back and do nothing to try and relieve them. Although it has become a modern cliché, I love the prayer that says, 'Lord, give me the serenity to accept the things I cannot change, courage to change the things I can, and wisdom to know the difference.'

We need to have the courage to change the things that we know we can. It is not a simple thing being the agent of change ourselves, when living with a current situation may not only be the acceptable, but the easier option. None of us like to be the one that rocks the boat, but often God uses difficult circumstances, and the tragic events that happen in life, to waken us up to a job he wants done, and is calling us to do! Some fine examples of this can be found in Michelle Guinness' book *Is God Good for Women?*

This sort of challenge brings us abruptly face to face with life's uncertainties, not knowing where a particular decision or course of action may lead us in the future—and it is difficult to live with life's uncertainties.

'Active' waiting, that which looks for God's preparation and work of change through adverse circumstances, helps us to deal with these uncertainties. As we watch and listen, our faith and strength is renewed and we become ready to rise to whatever God places in our path whenever it happens (Isaiah 40:31).

I do not know what the next year or the one after will hold for me. At the moment I have no idea what the Lord may be calling me to do in this next stage of life. I have come to a point where I have seen the futility of my own 'human' plans, and I am waiting for his guidance (Proverbs 16:1).

The last time I was faced with so many unknown possibilities was as a school leaver. Then I used to sing myself this song to help me remember to trust God for the future as well as the present. Although it comes from a song book nobody uses now, the words are still valid today! Perhaps you and I both can use them as a prayer as we face the future.

I do not know what lies ahead,
The way I cannot see,
But One is there who truly cares,
He'll show the way to me.

I know who holds the future, and he'll guide me with
                                              his hand.
With God things don't just happen, everything by him
                                              is planned.
So as I face tomorrow with its problems large and small,
I'll trust the God of miracles, give to him my all.

A.B. SMITH AND E. CLARK

Muddling along

An extract from The Way to Live
by Margaret Killingray

John and Peg are having a conservatory put on to the back of their house. Images of lovely spring evenings, sitting in the glow of the sunset, warm and comfortable after a busy day, fill them both with great pleasure. On their own with all their children gone, the planning and choosing of carpets, furniture and curtains make up for the slightly empty feel of a house that was once full of growing young people. The hassle of finding builders is over; the estimate is reasonable.

One morning the man in charge mentions to John that he would like to be paid in cash; it is apparent that he will not be paying income tax and is offering to avoid adding Value Added Tax to the bill. He is being generous and helpful to John and Peg as well as to himself.

Later that evening, John and Peg talk about the builder's request and wonder how they should respond. While they are talking, there is the sound of a key in the lock, and their youngest daughter walks in. She looks round at the nearly finished room, at the catalogues and curtain samples. She asks them why on earth they are spending so much money on themselves when there are empty bedrooms upstairs, homeless people on the streets, and beyond that a hungry and suffering world.

Caught off balance

John and Peg were taken by surprise, caught off balance by a builder they were employing and a daughter they had brought up. Each presented them with issues they had not even thought about; questions they had never asked. Of course, they knew that there were a hundred ways of not being quite straight in business dealings, and of course they knew that some people spend large amounts of money on high living and never give to needy causes. But on the whole they assumed, without thinking about it very much, that other people did those things and not them. Their immediate response to the builder was that only the government was losing out, that no person was being hurt, and if they refused to pay him cash they would be throwing his generous offer back in his face and making life difficult for themselves. They were a little affronted by a daughter's criticism when they remembered some of the trials she had put them through when she was growing up.

Like many of us, they could see the general principles, but found it hard to work out how to apply them in particular circumstances. They could believe that cheating, stealing and self-indulgence were wrong, and that generosity and fair play were right. But they were very unsure what those high-sounding moral values meant when it came to making decisions about their conservatory. Surely rules were meant to be bent, especially when it would be very difficult and embarrassing not to?

How would we respond to challenges like this? If we look back on our lives, how have we solved such problems? Perhaps at the time we were not even aware that we had made a decision. Many of us may not be too pleased with ourselves when we look back at some of the actions we have taken and the way we have behaved. In ordinary everyday living, we are glad that others cannot know about some of the things we have done.

There can be very few of us who have behaved exactly as we would have liked. If we had had time to think, or could have seen the issues more clearly in the first place, things might have worked out better. We often speak and act before we think. We are sometimes blinded by anger or love. Most of us are inconsistent, are not quite sure what the rights and wrongs are, when faced with a problem that has to be dealt with on the spot. Is it possible to be more prepared, to have a greater understanding of ourselves, other people and the world in which we live? Is it possible to learn how to make the right decisions and to do so more often? How can we find out what the right decisions are? In other words, how can we learn the best way to live?

Our heads contain a range of guidelines and rules. Some come from our upbringing, our parents and our schools; some come from the groups that we belong to; some from religious sources; some from television and the media. Some we keep. Some we don't. Some we keep one day, because we feel like it, and not another day because we feel mean and lousy. Most of us can harbour two contradictory rules at the same time— rather like making the Christmas pudding, muttering, 'Too many cooks spoil the broth' and 'Many hands make light work' at the same time.

Our changing world

Sometimes our problems with knowing what is wrong and what is right arise because our world is changing so fast that we are constantly facing new situations that do not fit into our existing ways of thinking. My husband's grandmother was a fierce old lady with very strong views about right and wrong. These included hair length and whether shirts were tucked into trousers. She spoke darkly about the evils of dancing, theatre and the cinema. When she was in her eighties, she moved to live with my mother-in-law and for the first time sat in a room with a television. She accepted it completely, watching everything that came on—sitcoms, fashion, pop programmes, cartoons, *Come Dancing*. She never said anything against it. It was something new. Her ideas about what was evil were already fixed and she could not see that television was similar to theatre and cinema. It made for a more peaceful house, but it highlights one of the problems we all face. When times change we don't always apply old rules to new situations.

Why do we sometimes not do what we know is right, and sometimes make a mess of our own lives, even though everyone else around us warned us it would happen? The answers to these questions can help us to be wiser and more understanding about ourselves and others.

Most of us do respond to the opinions of others, especially those whom we love and admire. In that way we may have some influence on our own circles of family, friends and col-leagues. I believe that living as a Christian is the way to dis-cover how to live a good life. There are, of course, large num-bers of people who live good and creative lives who are not Christians, and Christians who do not. But in a changing world, many are searching for a firm base for living, and are finding it increasingly difficult to keep to the patterns they think are right when such patterns are being challenged. Being a disciple of Jesus Christ does provide that firm base.

Christians are having to think afresh about their own ways of acting and think-ing as the world about them changes. Margaret Killingray's new book *The Way to Live* (Christina Press) sets out to bring some understanding and a wider vision to take us into the next thousand years!

Other Christina Press titles

Women by Design Penelope Swithinbank
£6.99 in UK
'God made us women and it was no accident,' writes the author.
'That's what he intended for you and me, with all the attendant
joys, excitements, challenges and problems of being a woman.
Whether you are a tomboy or a princess, he made you just the way
you are, because he loves you.' Yet many women secretly long to
be different in some way. This book sets out to help each of us to
be different by being free to be ourselves as women designed by
God. Penelope believes he chooses, calls and equips us to be
women of integrity and influence.

Who'd Plant a Church? Diana Archer
£5.99 in UK
Planting an Anglican church from scratch, with a team of four—
two adults and two children—is an unusual adventure even in
these days. Diana Archer is a Felixstowe vicar's wife who gives a
distinctive perspective on parish life.
   'An extremely gifted writer.' *Jennifer Rees Larcombe*

Pathway Through Grief edited by Jean Watson
£6.99 in UK
Ten Christians, each bereaved, share their experience of loss.
Frank and sensitive accounts offering comfort and reassurance to
those recently bereaved. Jean Watson has lost her own husband
and believes those involved in counselling will also gain new
insights from these honest personal chronicles.

God's Catalyst Rosemary Green
£8.99 in UK
The highly commended guide to prayer counselling.
   Rosemary Green's international counselling ministry has prayer
and listening to God at its heart. Changed lives and rekindled faith
testify to God's healing power. Here she provides insight, inspira-
tion and advice for both counsellors and concerned Christians
who long to be channels of God's Spirit to help those in need.
   God's Catalyst is a unique tool for the non-specialist counsellor; for the pastor who has no training; for the Christian who
wants to come alongside hurting friends.

'To read this book will be helpful to any Christian interested in helping others.' *John White*

Angels Keep Watch Carol Hathorne
£5.99 in UK

A true adventure showing how God still directs our lives, not with wind, earthquake or fire, but by the still small voice.

'Go to Africa.' The Lord had been saying it for over forty years. At last, Carol Hathorne had obeyed, going out to Kenya with her husband. On the eastern side of Nairobi, where tourists never go, they came face to face with dangers, hardships and poverty on a daily basis, but experienced the joy of learning that Christianity is still growing in God's world.

Not a Super-Saint Liz Hansford
£6.99 in UK

'You might have thought Adrian Plass... had cornered the market in amusing diary writing. Well, check out Liz Hansford's often hilarious account of life as a Baptist minister's wife in Belfast. Highly recommended.' *The New Christian Herald*

Liz Hansford describes the outlandish situations which arise in the manse, where life is both fraught and tremendous fun. *Not a Super-Saint* is for the ordinary Christian who feels they must be the only one who hasn't quite got it all together. The message is, 'You are not alone.'

The Addiction of a Busy Life Edward England
£5.99 in UK

Twelve lessons from a devastating heart attack. Edward, a giant of Christian publishing in the UK, and founder of Christina Press, shares what the Lord taught him when his life nearly came to an abrupt end. Although not strictly a Christina title (Edward lacks the gender qualifications), we believe you may want to buy this for the busy men in your lives.

'A wonderful story of success and frailty, of love and suffering, of despair and hope. If you are too busy to read this book, you are too busy.' *Dr Michael Green*

All the above titles are available from Christian bookshops everywhere, or in case of difficulty, direct from Christina Press using the order form on page 156.

Other Bible Reading Fellowship titles

Affirming Love Christine Leonard
Reflections into the heart of God
£5.99 in UK
Sets out to show God's love in its many aspects. *Affirming Love* interprets Bible passages through images, stories, poetry and meditations, to feed and stimulate the mind, senses, spirit and emotions, soaking us in the wonder of God's love, both in the normal course of life and in dark times. It aims to reach the hearts of many individuals who find it hard to know, deep down, that God really loves them.

Driven Beyond the Call of God Pamela Evans
Discovering the rhythms of grace
£7.99 in UK
A powerful new book that shows how, rather than presenting the Good News, 'church' can sometimes be very bad news indeed. Pamela Evans is a doctor with a background in medical research, and an accredited counsellor with a long-standing interest in process addictions. In this book she explores how Christians may find themselves driven towards burnout, becoming so absorbed in the process of worshipping and serving God that they lose sight of him altogether. Drawing on years of pastoral experience, she explores a right view of God and shows how his true requirements of us actually produce good mental and spiritual health. She shows, too, how we need an experience of his grace—a gift we cannot earn, however hard we try.

For 3–7 year olds:
Easy Ways to Christmas Plays Vicki Howie
£7.99 in UK
Contains three simple yet effective nativity plays suitable for use with groups of mixed ages. *Come to my party! The star who couldn't twinkle* and *Shine your lights!* All the children are involved in actions, mimes and songs throughout the play, with the speaking parts designed for older children in the group.

Each play is preceded by a complete story version of the play, with a five-week countdown to the performance including crafts, photocopiable activity sheets and scripts for each week running up to the performance. Suggested stage positions and photocopiable posters also included.

For 5–6 year olds:
On the Story Mat cassette Written and read by Brian Ogden
42 stories from the On the Story Mat range
£8.99 in UK (inc. VAT)
Meet Mrs Jolley and her reception class at Daisy Hill School in these delightful Bible stories, told especially for children in their early school years. Each story relates to a typical classroom incident, well within the experience of the young listener. With 18 stories from the Old Testament and 24 from the New Testament, *On the Story Mat* invites you to listen again and again to your favourite tales. Ideal for car journeys and bedtime or storytime use in the home, school or church. Running time approximately three hours.

For 7–11 year olds:
Toby and Trish and The Amazing Books of Mark/Jonah
Tom and Peggy Hewitt
£3.99 in UK
Husband-and-wife team Tom and Peggy Hewitt bring the Bible alive, enabling young readers to work systematically through individual books as a whole. Presented in an undated page-a-day format, each page has the key Bible verse printed out, with brief comment, illustration and prayer. Readers are invited to join the two characters Toby and Trish on an exciting journey of discovery through the books of Mark and Jonah.

All the above titles are available from Christian bookshops everywhere, or in case of difficulty, direct from BRF using the order form on page 157.

Christina Press Publications Order Form

All of these publications are available from Christian bookshops everywhere or, in case of difficulty, direct from the publisher. Please make your selection below, complete the payment details and send your order with payment as appropriate to:

Christina Press Ltd
Broadway House
The Broadway
Crowborough
East Sussex
TN6 1HQ

		Qty	Price	Total
8712	Women by Design	____	£6.99	____
8706	Who'd Plant a Church	____	£5.99	____
8705	Pathway Through Grief	____	£6.99	____
8700	God's Catalyst	____	£8.99	____
8703	Angels Keep Watch	____	£5.99	____
8708	Not a Super-Saint	____	£6.99	____
8709	The Addiction of a Busy Life	____	£5.99	____

POSTAGE AND PACKING CHARGES	UK	Europe	Surface	Air Mail
One book	£1.25	£2.25	£2.25	£3.50
Two books	£2.00	£3.25	£4.00	£5.50
Three/four books	£4.00	£5.50	£7.50	£11.00
More than four	free	prices on request		

Total cost of books £ _____
Postage and Packing £ _____
TOTAL £ _____

All prices are correct at time of going to press, are subject to the prevailing rate of VAT and may be subject to change without prior warning.

Name _____
Address _____
_____
_____ Postcode _____

Total enclosed £ _____ (cheques should be made payable to 'Christina Press Ltd')

 Please send me further information about Christina Press publications

DBDWG0399

BRF Publications Order Form

All of these publications are available from Christian bookshops everywhere, or in case of difficulty direct from the publisher. Please make your selection below, complete the payment details and send your order with payment as appropriate to:

BRF, Peter's Way, Sandy Lane West, Oxford OX4 5HG

		Qty	Price	Total
052	Affirming Love	____	£5.99	____
054	Driven Beyond the Call of God	____	£7.99	____
017	Easy Ways to Christmas Plays	____	£7.99	____
049	The Amazing Book of Mark	____	£3.99	____
055	The Amazing Book of Jonah	____	£3.99	____
081	On the Story Mat Cassette	____	£8.99	____

POSTAGE AND PACKING CHARGES				
order value	UK	Europe	Surface	Air Mail
£6.99 & under	£1.25	£2.25	£2.25	£3.50
£7.00–£14.99	£3.00	£3.50	£4.50	£6.50
£15.00–£29.99	£4.00	£5.50	£7.50	£11.00
£30.00 & over	free	prices on request		

Total cost of books £ _____
Postage and Packing £ _____
TOTAL £ _____

All prices are correct at time of going to press, are subject to the prevailing rate of VAT and may be subject to change without prior warning.

Name _____

Address _____

_____ Postcode _____

Total enclosed £ _____ (cheques should be made payable to 'BRF')

Payment by: cheque ❑ postal order ❑ Visa ❑ Mastercard ❑ Switch ❑

Card no. ☐☐☐☐ ☐☐☐☐ ☐☐☐☐ ☐☐☐☐

Card expiry date ☐☐☐☐   Issue number (Switch) ☐☐☐☐

Signature _____
(essential if paying by credit/Switch card)

❑ Please send me further information about BRF publications

Subscription information

Each issue of *Day by Day with God* is available from Christian bookshops everywhere. Copies may also be available through your church Book Agent or from the person who distributes Bible reading notes in your church.

Alternatively you may obtain *Day by Day with God* on subscription direct from the Publishers. There are two kinds of subscription:

Individual Subscriptions are for four copies or less, and include postage and packing. To order an annual Individual Subscription please complete the details on page 160 and send the coupon with payment to BRF in Oxford. You can also use the form to order a Gift Subscription for a friend.

Group Subscriptions are for five copies or more, sent to one address, and are supplied post free. Group Subscriptions run from 1 May to 30 April each year and are invoiced annually. To order a Group Subscription please complete the details opposite and send the coupon to BRF in Oxford. You will receive an invoice with the first issue of notes.

All subscription enquiries should be directed to:

BRF
Peter's Way
Sandy Lane West
Oxford
OX4 5HG

Tel: 01865 748227
Fax: 01865 773150
E-mail: subscriptions@brf.org.uk.

Group Subscriptions

The Group Subscription rate for *Day by Day with God* will be £9.00 per person until April 2000.

☐ I would like to take out a group subscription for _____ (Qty) copies.

☐ Please start my order with the January/May/September* 2000 issue
I would like to pay annually/receive an invoice with each edition of the notes*. (*Please delete as appropriate)

Please do not send any money with your order. Send your order to BRF and we will send you an invoice. The Group Subscription year is from May to April. If you start your Group in the middle of a subscription year we will invoice you for the remaining number of issues left in that year.

Name and address of the person organising the Group:

Name _____
Address _____
_____
_____
Postcode _____ Telephone _____
Church _____ Name of Minister _____

Name and address of the person paying the invoice if the invoice needs to be sent directly to them:

Name _____
Address _____
_____
_____
Postcode _____ Telephone _____

Please send your coupon to:

BRF
Peter's Way
Sandy Lane West
Oxford
OX4 5HG

DBDWG0399   The Bible Reading Fellowship is a Registered Charity

Individual Subscriptions

☐ I would like to give a gift subscription (please complete both name and address sections below)

☐ I would like to take out a subscription myself (complete name and address details only once)

The completed coupon should be sent with appropriate payment to BRF. Alternatively, please write to us quoting your name, address, the subscription you would like for either yourself or a friend (with their name and address), the start date and credit card number, expiry date and signature if paying by credit card.

Gift subscription name _____

Gift subscription address _____

_____ Postcode_____

Please send to the above for one year, beginning with the January/May/September 2000 issue:

	UK	Surface	Air Mail
Day by Day with God	☐ £10.50	☐ £12.00	☐ £13.50

Please complete the payment details below and send your coupon, with appropriate payment, to **The Bible Reading Fellowship, Peter's Way, Sandy Lane West, Oxford OX4 5HG.**

Your name _____

Your address _____

_____ Postcode_____

Total enclosed £ _____ (cheques should be made payable to 'BRF')

Payment by: cheque ☐ postal order ☐ Visa ☐ Mastercard ☐ Switch ☐

Card no. ☐☐☐☐ ☐☐☐☐ ☐☐☐☐ ☐☐☐☐

Card expiry date ☐☐☐☐ Issue number (Switch) ☐☐☐

Signature _____
(essential if paying by credit/Switch card)

NB: These notes are also available from Christian bookshops everywhere.